"Havin Guneser is not just the w[...]
on the thought of Abdullah Öc[...]
sensitive, and challenging rev[...]
a message the world despe[...]
—David Graeber, author of *Debt: The First
5,000 Years* and *Bullshit Jobs: A Theory*

"This book is a necessary contribution to the understanding
of a revolutionary movement that is very different
from the Eurocentric legacy of European and Western
revolutionary traditions. The science of women, or
jineology, is one of its contributions, one that both men
and women should understand to deepen our critique and
our anti-capitalist struggle, along with the concepts of
critique and self-critique and democratic confederalism."
—Raúl Zibechi, author of *Dispersing Powers: Social
Movements as Anti-state Forces* and *The New Brazil:
Regional Imperialism and the New Democracy*

"A bright light shining through the darkness of these
times, an extraordinary achievement in the most dreadful
conditions. We need to understand more about the struggle
for freedom being fought by the Kurdish movement. This
book by Havin Guneser is a clear, committed, inspiring, and
necessary introduction to the movement and its ideas."
—John Holloway, author of *Crack Capitalism* and *In, Against,
and Beyond Capitalism: The San Francisco Lectures*

"In this unmissable book, Havin Guneser strikes the
right chords with her uncompromising and warm-
hearted analysis of the Kurdish freedom movement
and the Kurdish women's movement. A must-read for
everyone who wants to understand what the struggle
for freedom means in today's violent world."
—Ana Cecilia Dinerstein, author of *The Politics of Autonomy in
Latin America: The Art of Organising Hope* and *Social Sciences
for an Other Politics: Women Theorizing without Parachutes*

KAIROS

In ancient Greek philosophy, *kairos* signifies the right time or the "moment of transition." We believe that we live in such a transitional period. The most important task of social science in time of transformation is to transform itself into a force of liberation. Kairos, an editorial imprint of the Anthropology and Social Change department housed in the California Institute of Integral Studies, publishes groundbreaking works in critical social sciences, including anthropology, sociology, geography, theory of education, political ecology, political theory, and history.

Series editor: Andrej Grubačić

Recent and featured Kairos books:

Asylum for Sale: Profit and Protest in the Migration Industry edited by Siobhán McGuirk and Adrienne Pine

Building Free Life: Dialogues with Öcalan edited by International Initiative

The Sociology of Freedom: Manifesto of the Democratic Civilization, Volume III by Abdullah Öcalan

In, Against, and Beyond Capitalism: The San Francisco Lectures by John Holloway

Anthropocene or Capitalocene? Nature, History, and the Crisis of Capitalism edited by Jason W. Moore

We Are the Crisis of Capital: A John Holloway Reader by John Holloway

Re-enchanting the World: Feminism and the Politics of the Commons by Silvia Federici

Autonomy Is in Our Hearts: Zapatista Autonomous Government through the Lens of the Tsotsil Language by Dylan Eldredge Fitzwater

The Battle for the Mountain of the Kurds: Self-Determination and Ethnic Cleansing in the Afrin Region of Rojava by Thomas Schmidinger

Crossroads: I Live Where I Like: A Graphic History by Koni Benson, illustrated by André Trantraal, Nathan Trantraal, and Ashley E. Marais

For more information visit www.pmpress.org/blog/kairos/

The Art of Freedom

A Brief History of the Kurdish Liberation Struggle

Havin Guneser

International Initiative Edition

KAIROS

PM

ISBN: 978-1-62963-781-5 (paperback)
ISBN: 978-1-62963-907-9 (hardcover)
ISBN: 978-1-62963-804-1 (ebook)
Library of Congress Control Number: 2019946089

Cover Image: "Şinperik" by Ercan Altuntaş, watercolor on canvas,
13 × 27 cm
Cover by John Yates / www.stealworks.com
Interior design by briandesign

10 9 8 7 6 5 4 3 2 1

PM Press
PO Box 23912
Oakland, CA 94623
www.pmpress.org

Printed in the USA.

Published with International Initiative Edition
International Initiative
"Freedom for Abdullah Öcalan – Peace in Kurdistan"
P.O. Box 100 511
D-50445 Cologne
Germany
www.freeocalan.org

Contents

Introduction

Andrej Grubačić

The Art of Freedom is undoubtedly the best introduction to the Kurdish liberation struggle available in the English language. One of the many virtues of this splendid book is that it is not focused exclusively on the revolutionary process in northeastern Syria. Rather, this remarkable revolutionary project has been carefully situated within the much broader and much longer history of the Kurdish freedom movement. But perhaps the strongest recommendation for spending time with this short book is the author herself. While it certainly may appear counterintuitive to insist on the significance of author in the context of the antiauthoritarian movement she so vividly describes, it would be a disservice to readers not to spend at least a moment on Havin Guneser. A friend and a *heval* (comrade) to many, Havin has been tirelessly, seemingly effortlessly, explaining and translating the political language of democratic modernity for people outside of the Middle East. For many of us, she has been a principal point of contact, a guide to the universe of astonishingly innovative political practices exemplified in the Rojava revolution. As a spokesperson for the International Initiative "Freedom for Abdullah Öcalan—Peace in Kurdistan," Havin has witnessed and been party to the important shifts and changes that inform and orient this book. Her informal presentation style makes these essays, originally lectures delivered in the auditorium of California Institute of Integral Studies in San Francisco, the partner institution of Rojava University, both direct and captivating—transporting the reader to the streets of Kobanî and Qamishli, as well as elaborating upon political meetings that took place in the Kurdish mountains. ("I love you as much as Apoist members love their meetings!" is a wedding vow one sometimes hears in Kurdistan). One could speak of "walking" through the history of the region with Havin, and it gradually becomes clear that in the course of all this walking, the author has become a comrade.

By meticulously reconstructing the history of the Kurdish struggle, Havin dispatches a number of persistent myths. Contrary to more than a few erroneous interpretations, the revolution in Rojava was not a spontaneous miracle or the product of an immaculate conception. It was a result of forty years of organizing. This "vision of free life," as Havin calls the organizational structures that were set up in prerevolutionary Syria, has not been easy to realize. As one of the cochairs of the canton of Kobanî said during my visit to that city, "The reason Kobanî still stands is precisely because we have built the structures of self-organization well before the ISIS attack." By the time Assad's army retreated from the northeast in 2012, the region was already organized in decentralized direct democratic committees—as an alternative to nation-state, this system is more accurately described as "democratic confederalism." One of the cornerstones of democratic modernity, democratic confederalism rests on principles of democratic nation, democratic politics, and communal self-defense.[1] Within this political context, accumulation of power and capital have been eradicated by the structures of a democratic, ecological, and gender-liberated society. The sociology of freedom replaces the sociology of the state, and the unit of both action and analysis returns to "moral and political society."

As one of the members of the *asayish*, the communal self-defense force, told me when I visited Qamishli: "My grandmother taught me what democratic confederalism is." Indeed, grandmothers are the very center of the Kurdish revolutionary project. Liberation of society—a project that Abdullah Öcalan calls "democratic civilization"—is possible only on the basis of liberation of women. A revolution must be feminist, or it is not a revolution. Women are "the first class, nation, and colony." Anti-colonial struggle begins with women's freedom; liberation of women is liberation of life (this is the meaning of the famous Kurdish political slogan *Jin, Jiyan, Azadi*). This, naturally, stands conventional socialist wisdom on its head, by redefining work to include the exploitation of the unpaid labor of women and nature.

In her lectures, Havin convincingly dispels the oft-repeated notion that Abdullah Öcalan is a leader in the traditional socialist sense. Öcalan, one of the most prominent political theorists of our time, has been a prisoner of the Turkish State since 1999. Held in strict isolation on the İmralı island, he is regarded by his comrades as a "*rêber*," or guide. Even though he was one of the founders of the PKK in 1978, he is not a leader in the conventional sense of the word. One of the most interesting aspects of the Kurdish politics is that it resists such complexity-flattening categories. At least since his imprisonment, and, Havin argues, well before that, Öcalan has used his authority to undermine authoritarian tendencies in the organization; and, as the "most loyal comrade," he had advocated for the "killing of the hegemonic male" and a feminist reorientation of the organization. In some thirteen books penned in prison as part of his many trials, he consistently urged the Kurdish freedom movement to liberate politics from the state, the nation from nationalism, and society from patriarchy. In a dialogue with the works of Murray Bookchin, Fernand Braudel, Immanuel Wallerstein, and Andre Gunder Frank, as well as with emancipatory aspects of the Kurdish tradition, Öcalan has developed a brilliant critique of capitalist modernity.[2] But this is where an important caveat is in order:

Öcalan's remarkable intellectual project is a creative synthesis of the forty-year experience of Kurdish revolutionary politics. Some of the most attractive aspects of his work were developed as a direct and impassioned response to active conversations taking place within the movement itself; it was the experience of Kurdish revolutionary women that had a decisive influence on Öcalan's new perspective, and it was his new perspective that had a decisive influence on the development of the new Kurdish politics.[3] On these and many other points, Havin brilliantly refreshes our understanding of the Kurdish freedom movement.

If the revolution in Rojava is neither a spontaneous event nor one scripted by a great leader, what is it really? Based on Havin's lectures, as well as my own observations while in the region, it seems as though new forms of Kurdish politics have so far proven to be a satisfying response to what Daniel Guerin has called the "problem of the revolution."[4] In his view, the problem has three aspects: the first one concerns the relationship between spontaneity and consciousness, between the masses and the leaders; the second asks what form of political and administrative organization should replace the bourgeois regime; and the third interrogates how the economy should be administered and by whom. Kurdish revolutionaries have proposed a synthesis of spontaneity and consciousness, insisting that we need to build the fact of the future in the present and organize in a way that by its very nature prefigures the democratic society.

As Havin states time and again, education is central to any revolutionary project. In Rojava, academies and universities are everywhere. As one of the members of the Department of Jineoloji—an important concept that this book will clarify— at Rojava University told me, "Democratic autonomy is not a one-day problem-solving exercise; it is an approach, a process, and a method." Autonomy is a collective practice; everything from political economy to local matters is discussed collectively. If Rojava is a revolution of life, education is seen as the revolution's most privileged aspect. Educational practices are not limited to formal spaces, however. Rather, people are educated in the street markets, meetings, councils, and committees. The ingenious practice of *tekmil* (roughly translated: report) brings to mind Rosa Luxemburg's important idea of apprenticeship in direct democracy.[5]

As concerns the political form, instead of the Leninist tentacular monster, Kurdish politics is premised on direct horizontal democracy and networked confederal structures. In the middle of the civil war in Syria, revolutionaries in Rojava have created a democratic nation, an autonomous region where Kurds, Arabs, Turkmen, Assyrians, Armenians, and Christians have instituted a nonethnic collective political structure of autonomous cantons run by councils, committees, and assemblies. This social contract represents one of the shining hours of modern history, a democratic confederation painstakingly pieced together over many years by delegates across Northern Syria. As Salih Muslim points out, this is essentially a democracy without a state.

And while the economy is still dominated by the immediate needs of war, most of the people with whom I spoke during my visit to Rojava were adamant about the need for autonomous management of common resources. There was very little sympathy for nationalization, and even less respect for the sanctity of private property. What remains to be worked out is a mechanism of harmonizing various interests in a new communal economy.

Walter Benjamin famously called statist politics "the foulest of all games this planet offers,"[6] a sentiment with which Kurdish revolutionaries would wholeheartedly agree. The main question before us today is whether or not we can create a new project of emancipation that escapes from the binary logic that compels us to choose between tradition and modernity, between returning to the past and accepting the present, between barbaric reaction and catastrophic progress, between authoritarian socialism and possessive individualism, and between obscurantism and bureaucratic rationalism? The new kind of revolutionary politics practiced by the Kurdish freedom movement provides the answer. It is not a matter of finding solutions to certain problems but of aiming at an overall alternative to the existing state of affairs, a different mode of life, a new (democratic) civilization. This book is both an example of and a contribution to this new kind of revolutionary politics.

Notes

1   A useful recent overview of the history of Kurds in northeastern Syria can be found in Harriet Allsopp and Wladamir van Wilgenburg, *The Kurds of Northern Syria: Governance, Diversity, and Conflicts* (London: I.B. Taurus, 2019); also see Michael Knapp, Ercan Ayboğa, and Anja Flach, *Revolution in Rojava: Democratic Autonomy and Women's Liberation in Syrian Kurdistan* (London: Pluto Press, 2016).

2   Readers interested in the so-called world-system(s) debates between Gunder Frank, Wallerstein, and Amin, should read Andre Gunder Frank and Barry Gills, *The World System: Five Hundred Years or Five Thousand?* (London: Routledge, 1996). For Braudel's notion of plurality of social times, see Fernand Braudel, *On History* (Chicago: University of Chicago Press, 1982).

3   The most comprehensive collection of Öcalan's works can be accessed at http://ocalanbooks.com. PM Press has published some of the seminal works by the author, including: *Capitalism and the Age of Unmasked Gods and Naked Kings: Manifesto of the Democratic Civilization*, vol. 2: (2021); *Sociology of Freedom: Manifesto of the Democratic Civilization*, vol. 3: (2020); *Beyond State, Power and Violence* (2021); the superb collection *Building Free Life: Dialogues with* Öcalan (2020).

4   Daniel Guerin, *For a Libertarian Communism* (Oakland: PM Press, 2017).

5   Rosa Luxemburg, *Reform or Revolution* (London: Pathfinder Press, 1973); originally published as *Sozialreform oder Revolution?* (1919).

6   Michael Löwy, "Revolution against 'Progress:' Walter Benjamin's Romantic Anarchism," *New Left Review* 1, no. 152 (July–August, 1985), accessed December 10, https://tinyurl.com/y5wh55wo.

Critique and Self-Critique—The Rise of the Kurdish Freedom Movement from the Rubble of Two World Wars

I'm really happy to be here. It's my first time in California. Of course, I'm trying to figure out where I am here in your midst, because the recent experience of the Kurds, which spans more than forty-five years, is one—as I was saying today to friends here—that requires intimacy to share. It hasn't been a very easy marathon. It has been a very difficult quest for freedom, and it has changed over time—whenever the Kurds thought they had reached a point, they saw that the point had moved. So the quest for freedom that started on the basis of something very physical and very identifiable, the oppression, colonization, and annihilation of Kurdish people, moved on from there to the point where it became a quest for freedom in general and a questioning of the very meaning of life.

It's not that easy to delve into the topic, because the Kurdish movement has gone through multidimensional experiences, especially when you consider the fact that it started in the 1970s, when capitalism had reached its peak and was going into decline, as well as going through several different periods in the world history of resistance and revolution—for example, real socialism collapsed. The Kurdish movement went through all of these times and ages and eras.

Let me tell you a little bit about myself, as that will put things into context. I have been with the International Initiative "Freedom for Abdullah Öcalan—Peace in Kurdistan" for the last twelve years. I'm one of its spokespersons, and I also translate the works of Abdullah Öcalan, who is the main strategist of Kurdish freedom and one of the founders of the Kurdistan Workers' Party (PKK). He has been in an island prison since 1999, for almost twenty years, incommunicado for three years now. For the last three years, we have had no idea what is happening to him on this prison island, or to three other inmates who are also in prison in relation to the Kurdish freedom struggle. I point this out, because over the next three days I will be mostly talking about the ideas of Abdullah Öcalan and of the Kurdish freedom movement in general.

I decided to title these talks in general "The Art of Freedom: The Theory and Practice of Democratic Modernity," because the Kurdish freedom movement and the Kurdish people see themselves as part of the wider universal struggle for the freedom of humanity, women, peoples, and workers over a period of five thousand odd years—maybe on the third day I will talk a little bit more about how, after forty-five years of struggle, "Kurdishness" is no longer only an ethnic identity. There are also terms coined by Abdullah Öcalan—*democratic modernity* and *democratic civilization*—that I will go into in more depth on the third day.

Today I would like to set the scene for that, because a lot of labor, effort, sacrifice, thinking, and rethinking went into the establishment of this movement and its changing quests until today. Therefore, today will be more about critique and self-critique—the method by which the Kurdish freedom movement was able to produce its own dialectic of development in terms of its ideology, its daily political positions, and its mid- and longer-term goals and policies, as well as how it was able to circumvent all the traps and pitfalls that existed for revolutionary movements, especially in the Middle East, and in Turkey in particular, particularly in relation to the issues involved in the colonization of the Kurdish people. I think for context it is very important to understand who the Kurds are, what their history is, and what the Kurdish freedom movement is and where it is coming from. These are very important issues. This is why we would like to talk about how the Kurdish freedom movement was born—from the rubble of two world wars—and maybe, as we go along over the next two days, we will talk about what Öcalan calls World War III, which is going on right now, and how it should be viewed, and, therefore, how we can situate what the Kurds are doing in the Middle East at the moment. I will also provide a bit of a perspective about that.

On the second day, we will slowly move to the soul of the paradigm. Any ideology can actually be corrupted, and we've seen that happen, yet that doesn't mean that they haven't contributed to the struggles for freedom of humanity around the world. However, these ideologies have not really been able to produce an alternative way of living and doing. This is why, on the second day, we will talk about the rebellion of the oldest colony: women.[1] In doing so, we will try to establish the nature of the soul of this paradigm. Then, on the last day, we will try to show the nature of society's defense mechanism against this in terms of its political and social structure. I will try to do all of that over the three days, and I hope that the questions you may have will help to further clarify the issues. As I've said, very many things have happened, and at times I may emphasize something too little or perhaps too much, but your questions may help to more satisfactorily expand upon the issues at hand.

Of course, as I said, it has been almost impossible for Kurdish people to develop a struggle that would have presented their truth, and the reason for that is actually pretty simple. It's because the land that they live on is divided among four nation-states, Iran, Iraq, Syria, and Turkey. Of course, the story gets a little more complicated, because the new structuring of the Middle East was the result of outside intervention. Capitalism, before and during World War I and World War II, but especially after it had for the most part completed the colonization process of European society, tried—and still tries—to change

3

the way of life of the people who are living under its system, and when it was successful, it began to expand outward. The struggle inside the capitalist countries, the struggle of working-class people resisting and organizing against capitalism or, as Sylvia Federici's work has shown in the case of women, the witch hunts, could also be seen as resistance and struggle against capitalism taking root within these societies.

Therefore, on the one hand, as this internal colonization was successful, this capitalist system, of course, began to spread and colonize and impose its political and social system everywhere else. This is when the story got a little more complex in the Middle East as well, because this meant that the former state structures, which were empires that were not actually based on one nation or one ethnic identity but were autonomous structures of different tribes or ethnic groups, etc. were deemed very backward. The new states, which we will call nation-states, which are a very important pillar of the capitalist system, began to be imposed everywhere.

When we look around the world, we see that their leaders are usually military personnel. That was the case in Turkey as well. Therefore, there were multiple struggles going on in the Middle East. On the one hand, you had different ethnicities rebelling and women resisting, and, on the other hand, you had the national middle class, which had also struggled to carve out a nation-state for itself, beginning to form. At the same time, the British, Soviet, and French interventions in the region had begun.

In the meantime, of course, all these interventions also tried to instrumentalize the different rebellions, whether Armenian, Assyrian, or Kurdish. This resulted in a very complicated picture. If you look at any history, transitional periods come with a lot of massacres. This was also the case in the making of the Turkish state. In short, during the World War I and World War II, we saw how the very attempt at nation-building meant that various peoples who did not fit the single

4

ethnicity of a nation-state were eliminated. Turkey is not alone in this continuing practice, which is why states are so comfortable doing it; they are compliant partners in crime in this regard. They can always say to each other, "You did it too." Have a look at all the state-building practices, whether in Germany, Italy, France, or elsewhere. No matter what country you look at, you can see that a lot of different peoples have been suppressed, oppressed, and massacred to allow for an overarching identity to be built, one that does not necessarily represent any of them.

This was a little bit more difficult in the Middle East, because it is the cradle of civilization. That is how it is described. It is also the place—Mesopotamia—considered the cradle of the state form itself, in Sumer to be specific. The embryo of the state was actually developed during the Sumerian era, five thousand or so years ago. Therefore, what we find is that there is a far-reaching tradition of different peoples developing as distinct and established communities. Therefore, the making of the nation-state in the Middle East has been much bloodier, and this bloodiness continues until today.

Take the case of the Armenian people and their accumulations and achievements. They have such a deep-rooted cultural and physical existence, in fact, a social existence, that you can't just assimilate them and deem them nonexistent. Thus, the only avenue open is genocide or forced displacement, options that have been used. In Turkey and Greece, for example, there has been reciprocal forced displacement—sending the Turks back to Turkey, but mostly, of course, sending Greeks back to Greece, which included looting their belongings and lynching them—so this wasn't simple or without its pain and sorrow.

The Kurds, for their part, participated in the "independence war" that led to the formation of Turkish Republic spearheaded by the military field marshal Mustafa Kemal —and he was actually tactically and politically pretty proficient, as he was able both to establish relationships with Lenin and to later broker a deal with Britain, as well as with Germany from the period of the Ottoman Empire onward. Germany was a very ardent supporter of the Ottoman Empire and has continued to support the subsequent Turkish state. Germany was actually responsible for strengthening the militaries of both the Ottoman Empire and the Turkish Republic.

Although the early years of Turkish Republic included Kurdish representatives in the Turkish Grand Assembly, the republic quickly moved to suppress the Kurdish identity and to enforce the harshest interpretation of capitalism's nation-state based on a single ethnicity/culture, religion, and language. At the time—as is the case today—this was almost always based on the fear of an intervention by "foreign powers" and the fall from grace of the Ottoman Empire, which justified any and all oppression and exploitation and demanded the compliance of the entire political spectrum, from the left to the right.

Come the 1950s, 1960s, and 1970s, the situation, especially in terms of the Kurds, reached a point where there was no room left for much imagination. The Kurds had witnessed the genocides and massacres of the Armenians and the Assyrians and had seen what happened to the Greeks and the people in the Pontus region. Of course, one must add that some Kurds, particularly the Kurdish elites, became partners in crime with the Turkish rulers and governments, in the Armenian massacre in particular, in return for increased authority and greater wealth. This layer further complicates matters. Why do I say complicates? Because the rulers of each ethnicity worked together in an attempt to destroy the possibility of coexistence between peoples. So when you look at the history of the Middle East—maybe elsewhere as well, but we are looking at the Middle East right now—you see these sorts of layers and multidimensional developments. This makes it very difficult to begin imagining what might have been, because the picture that I'm drawing was not only a result of what Turkey, Iraq, Iran, and Syria did; it was actually also an imperial project.

Therefore, when you examine it, it becomes clear that these states were simultaneously subject to colonization in some way, while at the same time colonizing both other people and their own people.

What has been of constant importance for Öcalan and the Kurdish freedom movement has been to grasp how to live a meaningful life, while trying to recover and interpret the knowledge, or truth, of the Kurdish people. It's been a huge struggle, because, in the 1970s, when Kurds began to identify as a group, there was not much information about what was actually happening. By then, the Turkish state believed the process of assimilation of the Kurds had reached its end. On September 19, 1930, a newspaper in Turkey published a caricature, a tombstone on Mount Ararat that read: "Imaginary Kurdistan is buried here." With this caricature, they symbolized what they had actually done in the aftermath of a rebellion that ended in a massacre—or, rather, after two centuries of rebellions, as the Ottoman military records indicate, followed by several more specifically after the prohibition of Kurdish identity that followed the securing of the Turkish Republic.

I would say, imagination was a key element in the formation of this freedom movement. Under such circumstances, they were brave enough to imagine that things could be different. This bravery was, of course, the result of a couple of things. One was that at the time the Turkish left was very strong, and it had some very good leaders who actually acknowledged the existence of the Kurdish people and the importance of coexistence as equals, people like Deniz Gezmiş, İbrahim Kaypakkaya, and Mahir Çayan. They were exemplary people in this regard, and they influenced Abdullah Öcalan and the others involved in forming the early group. The Vietnamese national liberation movement was another factor that deeply affected the movement. And, of course, the 1968 movement that captured the imagination of the world also influenced these young people, who were mostly but not entirely students.

In these early days of the movement when they were just becoming a group, along with imagination, the people who got involved with the group and the way they slowly built themselves was also important. It was not only Kurds who made up the early group. There were, for instance, people from the Black Sea region and women and other people from different religious, class, and ethnic backgrounds. It was a mix of different people. Perhaps this Kurdish national liberation movement—because there were and still are others—did not fall into nationalism or sexism due to these elements in its early days and because, even as a group formation and in the founding members of the PKK, there was a plurality, thereby modeling the fact that coexistence without the denial of the other was possible.

Let me sum up what I am going to talk a little bit about—just to put it in perspective. In the early 1970s, we had the first grouping of the PKK. Then, in 1978, this group decided to have a founding congress in a small village. I think the details are important. They founded the PKK in a village in a very poor house, with twenty-two people present. They did not begin an armed struggle until 1984. In fact, if we look at the interventions that continued to occur in the Middle East, focusing on Turkey to see the contours of those interventions, we can see that the military coup in 1971—a US-led intervention—was primarily directed at the Turkish left. Let's not forget any of that.

As I said, the 1971 coup was primarily directed at the Turkish left, and, in the end, this led the Turkish left to increasingly fall into nationalism and to generally see the Kurdish freedom movement as untrustworthy and nationalist. During the military coup those leaders in the Turkish left who had a radical left perspective, including about the Kurdish issue, were killed or executed.

The 1980 coup more directly targeted the Kurdish movement, which was spreading and gaining support extremely quickly. As you can see, developments unfolded rapidly. In 1973, you have the early grouping. Then, in 1978, the organization is founded. And two years later there is a military coup. So before this movement can actually find its feet, one of the worst military coups in Turkish history happens. By 1979, Öcalan had seen this coming, so he had called upon most of the cadres to leave Turkey. Some left, and some didn't.

The Kurdish left, the PKK and its cadres, and the Turkish left, were subjected to mass arrest. These were very difficult years. This, as you perhaps know, was accompanied by brutal torture. I remember Sakine Cansiz, I don't know if you've heard of her; she was assassinated in 2013, in Paris. When she watched *Hunger*, the film about Bobby Sands, she said, "Yes, they did exactly the same things to us." Therefore, the savageness of the torture and the aim of this military coup, to crush any desire for freedom, was immense. These were very difficult years in that sense. Part of the movement left the country, while others were arrested and severely tortured, with the hope that, with so many people in prison, the movement would surrender and be entirely corrupted.

There were two important forms of resistance to this attempt. One was under Öcalan's leadership in what is now Rojava. Kobanî. . . maybe you've heard of Kobanî in 2015, but Öcalan, among others, first went to Kobanî in 1979, when he left Turkey. He stayed there and organized, before moving on to Lebanon. They got in touch with the PLO, organized and educated themselves in the PLO's camps in the Beqaa Valley and prepared to build a movement.

At around the same time, those who had been captured and those who were prisoners of war waged immense resistance in the prisons against the savagery and the attempt to totally destroy the newly forming PKK. This development of resistance was, of course, very much complemented by the actions of Öcalan and his comrades and the way they built the movement in Lebanon and elsewhere. When they saw the situation in the prisons and in the country, they determined that an armed struggle was necessary. The military coup left no room for a political approach. The aim of the state was to totally anni-hilate Kurdish existence, especially one that was left-wing. So, from 1978 to 1984, over a six-year period, the conditions for an armed struggle were established and, in 1984, it was declared.

It proved a very successful undertaking. At that time, the Kurds tended to describe the guerrillas, as "ten meters tall with two-meter-long weapons," which, of course, was not the case. The reason the guerrilla became so mythical was that the Turkish state had become such a crushing force that the people thought that nobody could act against them. I am talking about the events of August 15, 1984. This date marks the start of the armed resistance against imperialism, colonialism, and occupation in Kurdistan. This sudden action taken at two military posts in Northern Kurdistan was a sort of rejuvena-tion, because at that time the Kurdish people were presumed dead, totally incapable of reviving themselves, especially in Northern Kurdistan—thus, it is known as the day of revival among the Kurds. This date is significant because it is a turning point, because it seemed so unlikely and so impossible. Or, if it happened, it would not last. The state would crush it in a week or a month. The Kurdish people and the guerrilla saw that the coercive power of the state was not omnipotent; it could collapse. Until then, the situation that had been imposed on the Kurds was such that even a night guard without a weapon would have had power over the Kurds.

This is the dialectic of oppression and exploitation, and it has a psychological counterpart. Consider this: there was a case of domestic violence within the Kurdish community in dias-pora. I said to this physically huge woman—she was Kurdish, and she was being beaten by her husband, a very short man—if you just go like this [making a motion of holding his arm off], he won't be able to do anything to you. But she could not—at least not at first. Clearly most of this oppressive situation is ideological and psychological, and this was the exact situation the Kurdish people found themselves in. I will address this in more detail tomorrow.

Öcalan argues that all forms of slavery mimic women's slavery. The Kurds experienced numerous massacres and a ban on their language and culture—even the words *Kurds* and *Kurdistan* were banned in Turkey. You couldn't say *Kurds* or *Kurdistan*, and, for a long time, if you did, you had to say or write *K...*, without spelling it out in full. As such, the system had been shaped such that after a while the state did not even need soldiers with guns, because just a guard would be enough for a submissive and self-censoring life to prevail. Again, this is why the slow but very steady development of this freedom movement brought back trust, brought back the confidence of the Kurdish people in themselves and gave them back their dignity.

The PKK declared its first unilateral cease-fire in 1993, and one could say that this was the very first step away from interpreting self-determination in terms of a united socialist *state* of Kurdistan. This is also the earliest point at which talks became an option. Then President of Turkey Turgut Özal took a first step in this direction, but it fell apart when he died. Many people believe he was killed, some even believe that this was the case because some of the imperialist states did not want talks to go ahead. Even the Kurdish people, including PKK sympathizers thought this was a tactical move—perhaps because the break with interpreting the right to self-determination in terms of having a separate state had not yet occurred—but Öcalan made it clear that this was a genuine undertaking. This was followed by a series of unilateral cease-fires. Then, in 1998, there were a series of interventions in the Middle East. It's said that Bill Clinton, president at the time, spoke to Hafiz Esad twice. In 1998, Turkey sent its army to the border to Syria and demanded that Syria turn Öcalan over to Turkey. I'm really skipping around and jumping over things, to make the connections, and I hope it all makes sense. If not, let's talk about it a little bit more after the presentation.

Öcalan says that in 1998 an Israeli envoy visited him in Damascus and conveyed to him that if he accepted Israeli patronage regarding the Kurdish question, things could be different. Öcalan says that he neither found it morally nor politically correct to accept this. We do not know exactly what "this" is, because he doesn't really go into it. We can, however, see from unfolding events and incidents what "this" is. As was the case for Armenia, the idea is that a small Kurdistan in the north of Iraq represented by the Partiya Demokrat a Kurdistanê (Kurdistan Democratic Party; KDP), with the Yekîtîya Niştimanîya Kurdistan (Patriotic Union of Kurdistan; PUK) as their partners would be acceptable, and all the other parts would be sacrificed to and for this. Öcalan disagreed. He said, "I can't accept this," after which we saw a very quick succession of events.

In response to the increasing pressure being brought to bear on Syria, Öcalan decided to leave Syria on October 9, 1998. He said at the time that despite his attempts the Syrian state would not adopt a strategic friendship and a strategic approach to the Kurdish issue. He went to Europe instead of going to the Kurdish mountains, in hope that there might be a way to achieve a democratic political and peaceful solution to the Kurdish question.

I have to explain something else, because all these factors will determine how we locate what is going on in the Middle East. In 1981–1982, when the Kurdish freedom movement was training at the PLO camps in the Beqaa Valley, in Lebanon, there was, as you know, an attempted Israeli invasion. At the time, during the invasion, the PKK fought alongside the Palestinians to prevent the invasion, and there were thirteen PKK martyrs and some fifteen Kurdish POWs taken by Israel at the time. They were released much later.

Despite the fact that the Kurdish freedom movement itself is in a very tight and difficult spot, it has never held back support for other peoples' struggles. It didn't just take its own interests to heart but also looked at what was the best political approach in a given situation for the benefit of all peoples in the area, not just the Kurds. Thus, when we look at Öcalan and the movement's praxis in the different stages of its development, we can understand why Öcalan would be unwilling to accept Israeli patronage for the Kurdish question, finding it politically and morally unacceptable.

In 1998, when the odyssey of both Öcalan and the Kurdish people began, the Kurdish people were actually very responsive. This was both a historical period and the point at which the relationship between Öcalan, the PKK, and the Kurdish people across the world was shaped. It is a tried and tested relationship. It is a relationship in which they grew together from obscurity, from nonexistence. Let's put it that way. They grew together, because to suggest that this movement or Öcalan or anyone else knew everything from day one would be an extreme exaggeration. What happened is also relevant for our topic today—critique and self-critique. Their beginning point was a single sentence: "Kurdistan is a colony." From there they grew.

The PKK began as a Marxist-Leninist organization, which was an extremely bad thing to do at the time, because not only was Kurdishness already prohibited, banned, and deemed nonexistent, there was also the Cold War. So it was a total no-no. The Yalta agreement between the Soviet Union and the United States of America, dividing the world between them, was, however, even worse. Basically, the Soviet Union stopped supporting national liberation movements. So you've got it all in a nutshell. Like a Molotov cocktail, you've got all of the necessary bits that you shouldn't have.

In 1998, when Öcalan went to Europe, the international community of nation-states passed him around from one state to another. First, he went to Greece, followed by a back and forth to Russia, returning to Greece, then going on to Italy, then back to Russia, and finally back to Greece. The Greek state and its government at the time said they would take him to South Africa but, instead, they took him to Kenya. By *they* I mean a NATO operation that included the CIA, the Mossad, and their leading players. He was told that he was on a plane to South Africa, but he was, in fact, brought to Kenya, where he was abducted and handed over to the Turkish officials at the Nairobi Airport. Of course, there was a huge outcry from Kurds across the world. In fact, with this Kurdish outcry, Öcalan, who until then had been a leader of the PKK and one of the founders of the PKK, became a leader for the Kurdish people and their struggle for dignified self-determination across the world. The historical lesson was that every time a leader of a rebellion was arrested, he would then be executed, and the state would massacre people. This was a historical lesson drawn from the past twenty rebellions in Turkey and how they ended.

In Öcalan, Kurds saw what might befall them once again. On the one hand, they had a very tested relationship, because you can imagine the sorts of difficult periods and stages that Öcalan had steered them through, all the traps and difficulties that they faced. On the other hand, there was the historical experience that after a rebellion is crushed, a genocide follows. Therefore, Kurds everywhere, in the four parts of Kurdistan, in the US, in Australia, in Europe, everywhere, basically didn't go home. Even Madeleine Albright had to make a statement at the time. She said something to the effect of "oh my God, we didn't expect such a reaction from the Kurds."

This, of course, turned Öcalan into the leader of the majority of the Kurds, because the Kurds themselves embraced him. In his submission to the court in Athens, he said, "I had to strip myself of personal feelings of dignity. I had to think very hard about what to do next." Because he was, of course, also very much aware of the historical consequences, and he said that the nation-states bet on the fact that no one in the world—by which I mean no state or NGO or the UN—would chase up what happened to him. Who would chase up what is happening to the Kurds? Who would care? For instance, in the case of the Palestinian question, you have around twenty Arab countries that use the Palestinian question in their own domestic and external politics. They manipulate it for their own interests, but, nonetheless, this puts the Palestinian question on the agenda. Nothing like this is happening with the Kurdish question. Let me give you an example: today there is a huge conflict between Iran and Turkey, but to preserve the status quo, especially in the case of the Kurdish question, they can be buddies. They can act together hand in hand. The Kurds being divided into four parts is a trap for these four countries as well. It doesn't allow them to move forward either. They are always pulling each other down to keep this question unresolved. This is why Öcalan says that nobody would have wondered what really happened. Therefore, he says, "I was compelled to think it through and act responsibly." As a result, there were a lot of people who took to the streets in protest; they were sleeping on the streets of Rome on cold winter nights, and some of them even self-immolated. It was for him, but, at the same time, it was actually for themselves, as they knew what was going to happen. Öcalan, however, called on everybody to stop.

At the show trial on the island of İmralı, where he has now been held since 1999, instead of doing what was expected of him, he did something else; he came up with new ideas. These new ideas were presented in an atmosphere and ambiance of state-orchestrated lynching. Instead of doing something else, he came up with the idea of a democratic republic and presented it to the people. He tried to turn people away from violence back to ideas—not only the protesting Kurds but also the Turkish nationalists. Everybody was shocked, because, you know, everybody was expecting something else from him. Some people were expecting him to go on a hunger strike or kill himself in prison. Others were expecting him to surrender to the state. When he began doing the things he did, it was outside of the binaries that were possible. Afterward, as his approach was increasingly understood, trust in him and even more so in his strategic thinking and foresight, as well as a vision of what might come, grew, as did his ability to come up with new ideas—about which we will speak in more in depth in the upcoming sessions.

From 1999 to 2005, there was another period of reorientation. It marked a complete break with the whole of classical civilization and patriarchy. From 1993 to 1998, there had been attempts and efforts to rebuild the organization. As I mentioned at the beginning, this was, among other things, a reaction to the collapse of the Soviet Union. In the 1980s, feminism was at its apex, and it affected everybody, including the PKK, but it was unable to influence society at large, and it dwindled. During the lifetime of the PKK, all of the real socialist experiences or alternative movements came to a standstill. This is another layer that I want to emphasize. Instead of giving up the idea, especially after 1993, the movement began to really pose the question: Why? What was being done wrong? Critiquing it and critiquing themselves. Learning from the different movements around the world was also a very important part of all of this.

Öcalan responded extensively to these questions. Have I mentioned that he has put out more than sixty books, thirteen of them written on the island of İmralı as court submissions? In the midst of everything happening in the world politically, after the collapse of the real socialist countries, Öcalan, in the late 1990s, produced an analysis that specified that "to insist on socialism is to insist on being human." When patriarchal traits were becoming more prominent or, rather, exposed to an even greater degree, in 1996, he developed an analysis that later became a book titled *Killing the [Dominant] Man*. All this to say that there were many attempts at this time, but the clear rupture, after a series of developments, of course, came after 1999, when, from 1999 to 2005, he broke with the idea of the state completely. His books show his arguments and the thinking that went into making that rupture. I think after this the pieces began to fall into place. That is why later we will delve much further into what he calls democratic civilization and how he went back and evaluated history.

I will now make a bold jump forward to 2011, to the Rojava revolution, which is based on these ideals. We cannot separate the revolution in Rojava from the ideological and political developments of the past forty-five years. It didn't come out of thin air. On the contrary, it was based on all of the labors and organizational efforts of the previous forty-five years, including in Rojava at the time. I think now is the time to look at the Kurdish freedom movement's history from the perspective of the idea and practice of critique and self-critique. I think this is very important, because we really need to understand a little bit about the dialectics of the PKK's constant evolution and self-renewal, because some people would like to think that all these changes occurred because Öcalan was abducted, so he came up with a pragmatic idea. That is not what happened. We talked about the changes in the world over those forty-five years and their influence on this movement and, of course, how the movement's own struggle surfaced and gave rise to new knowledge and made manifest new aspects of the truth.

We are made to think of world history in a very linear way. For example, we only look at the struggle of the working class under capitalism, so we don't see the struggle of, let's say, the colonized people or tribes and clans that are resisting being sucked into classical civilization as just as important as the struggle of the working class. Another example would be that of women and their resistance to assimilation into this classical civilization. The fact is that all these different struggles have exposed aspects of this larger truth. What Öcalan is actually trying to do with his theory of democratic civilization and democratic modernity is to bring all this together as the integral truth, as the whole truth.

The Kurdish movement knew that all it had was a critique. As I said, they began by saying, "Kurdistan is a colony." So what they did at the beginning was recover Kurdish people's truth. Öcalan used to say, "Ninety-five percent of our struggle is against the Kurds. Only 5 percent is against the Turkish state." This is an immense reality, because over so many years of so many different policies—ideological, physical, and economic policies—the Kurds had distanced themselves from their own reality, and it was very difficult to bring them back to it. Öcalan would say, "Vietnamese people knew they were Vietnamese." But Kurds, you had to first say, "Hey, look, you have another truth! You have something else here." To be able to do that, they began with a critique; they had to expose the official state ideology of Turkey and the methods used by the state. What were those methods? They made some places extremely religious. They actually actively did that. And, in other places, they paved the way for high university attendance in specific cities. Let's say I'm from a specific city called A, I would be educated and would look down on everyone else, even though we would all be equally oppressed, exploited, and so on. This was an active expression of assimilationist policies. They used all sorts of different methods and techniques to make it very difficult for the people to associate, unite, and act together.

This clearly shows the infrastructure and superstructure of these methods, but I think what was even more important, and this is also another way that the freedom movement addressed this, was how these structures can be overcome— not just exposing these structures but also coming up with creative means to overcome them. In fact, the method was as follows: if you had a critique, you also had to show what the alternative was and why. So the other side of the coin of any critique was to show what the *new way* could be, what it is to be replaced with. Especially during those early years, the ideological and political capacity and ability of the movement was due to the dialectics of critiquing. What occurred as these critiques developed? One of the people who was present at the beginning said in an interview, "We would go to the villages and would say, 'Down with imperialism and the colonizers!' And then we would go away, but nothing would come down." So, although, yes, they critiqued it and talked about it, they saw by just talking they weren't bringing anything down. What had to follow, therefore, was the implementation and the practice of their theory.

From the group's birth to 1980s, the very important and primary task was to develop an ideological critique. There was not much self-critique yet, because they were still trying to find themselves: who they were, what they were trying to represent, what they rejected. The reason for this was very simple; they first had to break down the boundaries in their heads. Right? I don't know, maybe some of you tutor or give lessons. When you talk about something, you actually overcome yourself in a sense as well. All the other duties at the time were actually secondary. Therefore, what they did was analyze the situation, critique it, and take responsibility for doing something about it. I think today this dialectic is the motor force of the Kurdish freedom movement. In this period, some monumental works were written by Öcalan and his friends, including *Kürdistan'da Zorun Rolü* (The Role of Force in Kurdistan, 1983), which unfortunately has not been translated into English yet.

Of course, the movement went through many stages. Although critique was a constant part of the freedom movement's development, what they discovered when they tried to implement the results of their critique, was that they were not necessarily all doing the same thing. Some people had interpreted it in one way, others in another way. As a result, they realized that the time had come to turn the critique inward, and that is what they began to do. During this period, they critiqued Kurdish society from 1981–1982 onward, but especially the period following 1985. The critical focus became more internal than external. Their focus was both Kurdish rebellions of the past (the PKK was very much criticized for this, with people asking, "How can you criticize the rebellions?")

and Kurdish society, but they also critiqued themselves, their implementation efforts, and their practice.

They realized that two things were happening, the intellectuals and people coming from universities basically thought, "I will just tell the truth, and the rest will just follow," but how do you implement that. So that was critiqued. Others thought that there was no need for education, no need to expand knowledge, theory, or intellectualism. "We've made a decision. Now let's do it. That's all there is to it." Therefore, there was a lot of discussion to address these problems. They concluded that in their own praxis, practice could not be severed from theory or ideology. Their main pillar became, as Öcalan describes it, "Think as you do, and do as you think." This approach renders individuals totally open to doing things differently and to treat that moment of doing to act or respond differently than we had learned to. We usually act and react in predictable ways. If I slap you, you will slap me. Maybe that's a very vulgar way of presenting it, but if you slap me, I could pause to think about it and perhaps do something a little bit different. This approach was implemented both on the level of the immediate and on the level of praxis over longer periods of times—one year, a couple of months, whatever. This weapon of critique and self-critique allowed the movement to both clarify its position and determine how to implement it.

Finally, the concept and practice of critique and self-critique doesn't unfold on the basis of an individual's ideas. It unfolds on the basis of a paradigm or a political and ideological line that is accepted by an organization's members. Therefore, how an individual implements that line is evaluated. That individual is not evaluated on the basis of someone else's likes or dislikes or that person's own likes or dislikes. It's about a line, a paradigm, a set of ideas that have been collectively developed and consensually approved. Therefore, it doesn't leave any room for unclear motives and establishes a very transparent framework for all participants. At the same time, it allows for the further development of this ideological line. This is why the Kurdish freedom movement is not stuck forty-five years in the past. It has continually evolved, and it has based that evolution on very concrete factors, which it has laid out in its publications.

We will delve further into those factors tomorrow, because I think the way this rupture was made is very important, as is the way the movement was able to arrive at the truth and see itself as part of this struggle and quest for freedom. To return to the title of this lecture series, I think this is what makes it all so artistic. They did not mimic the system by taking the easy way out and saying, "No, no, we want our own state too." More on this tomorrow. Thank you for listening so patiently.

Q: *Based on what you were just talking about—this critique and self-critique—I wonder what the practical lived reality of that is like. How many hours a week on average do Kurdish radicals spend in meetings? I'll tell you something, there is no culture of hanging out at political meetings left in the Bay Area—hardly at all. It's at a low ebb and has been ebbing lower and lower over time, and I think it is part of the technological world that we're living in. Everybody is in this massive speedup, and everybody is too busy. Everybody is working all the time and paying all this ridiculous rent, etc. So I'm just really curious about the practical reality, starting with this epic break in 2005. You talked about it as a line or a sort of philosophical guide, some kind of parameters that were arrived at through collective discussion. In reality, how many hours per week do people spend doing that? And how does that actually work? Because it's hard for me to imagine having enough time to sit around with a bunch of people to come to those kinds of conclusions.*

Havin: Yes, I think one of the other things that the capitalist system has done is hijack our time. When we look at other state forms, we see that if we go back to the Roman Empire. . . a friend has done the research, so I had a look at what kind of holiday periods they had, and half of the days of the year were holidays—really. What the capitalist system says is: "If you don't work, you're a bum. And to avoid being bums everybody should work." And, even if not, you would not afford housing and other needs. Therefore, our time outside of work has been constantly reduced. Of course, this is part of the consumption culture, and work has been detached from meaning, but it's also so we don't have time to think or do anything constructive. Well, it would actually probably be seen as destructive. In the past, let's say, to have a shoemaker make you a pair of shoes, you would go to him or her and say, "I want a pair of shoes," and then return in a week. He or she could make the shoes in a day or two, or maybe a week. Now, people have to work nonstop making shoes, making this or that, and we have to work nonstop to consume what they make. We have lost control of time. You're right.

What happens is meetings become cumbersome, and talking becomes a burden. And we no longer have time for it. The real things that people should be doing become unnecessary things, because we are made to think and feel that it's easier if somebody else decides for us. So much easier! We don't have any responsibility, but we can criticize them for not doing the right thing. We are being reduced to that. I will talk more about this—probably tomorrow and the third day. Öcalan calls this *societycide,* he talks about this a lot in his book titled *The Sociology of Freedom.* Societycide. We will delve further into that.

We were in Rojava about three months ago, and I heard a story that was just too funny. Two people were getting married, and they asked the woman, "Do you like him? Do you love him?" She turned around and said, "I love him like the Apoists love their meetings." It's exactly what you've been asking about. It's not just the cadres—of course, there is a difference, and maybe if there is a question or if we get to talk about that, we can talk about who and what the cadres are. But, yes, not only the movement but the people too are always in meetings. There is no unnecessary work. This is so extremely important. I talked a little about critique and self-critique, but you begin to agree by gathering and talking and assessing, by evaluating and reevaluating what you are doing. It is an immense space of education.

When Abdullah Öcalan was in Damascus and in the Beqaa Valley, they would have huge educational sessions, and there would be anywhere from two to three hundred people: women, men, both cadres and ordinary people. They would all discuss together about political developments, about the revolutionary movement's praxis and cadres. And they wouldn't stop there. They would videotape the meeting and all of the discussions and send copies of the video to the homes of sympathizers, so the whole society could watch it. It was an amazingly open process of critique and self-critique that did not aim to discredit any individual but to make sure that all individual and collective practice would serve the development of the entire society, so that the whole society could overcome shared shortcomings. In the final analysis, all of these individuals are products of society, which is the product of the policies of various governments—not only that but that as well. Therefore, meetings are extremely important and are where the transformation of the mindset occurs for the Kurdish freedom movement.

This is, of course, extremely difficult, especially in the US, but everywhere else as well, because we are disabled from doing this by the fact that we must provide three basic things for ourselves: housing, food, and the needs associated with reproduction, the needs of children and the family. To survive, in this modernity everybody needs money. Something that is also discussed outside of Kurdistan is: How do you sever ties with wage slavery, so that you can actually do what you should be doing instead of just trying to survive? It's a very military thing, isn't it? I know in the Turkish military, at least it used to be, for example, when the leaves fell in autumn, the soldiers had to clean them up. It's a nonstop thing, the falling leaves. The soldiers used to be sent out to collect the falling leaves, so that they were not idle, so that they always had something to do. The same idea is implemented throughout society. "You should not be idle, so that you don't think. You should not start doing things." Therefore, we need to continuously open space for that, and we have to find ways to do that. Maybe we will talk about that on the second and third days—about how the freedom movement envisions doing that, because it's a very important point.

Q: *It seems to be that some sort of "rupture" has happened in the dynamics of armed struggle and cease-fires. Can you talk a little bit more about that, given the strong and important connection between the state apparatus and military apparatus? As the PKK was developing a theory and practice in this kind of ongoing consensus and engagement with civilians, what aspects of the armed struggle, historically or ideologically, changed and how?*

Havin: There were different influences. Cease-fires triggered a reimagining of the nature of self-determination and how to reinterpret it. Before that point, Öcalan found the issue of the state very mind-boggling. Because all of the other socialist and communist movements or national liberation movements ended up seizing state power. These practices showed us that they didn't take over the state; they were taken over by the state. As to the anarchists, Öcalan criticizes them for failing to offer much in the way of social and political organization of the community. At this juncture, the armed struggle becomes very important, because it has always been available to both revolutionary movements and states. Increasingly, states have monopolized the use of violence. This is one way they have left the people defenseless—by monopolizing violence, by legitimizing the idea that they alone should monopolize violence. What are you supposed to do, in the case of the Kurds, for example, when there are massacres, genocides, and involuntary assimilation? This is happening as we speak, and the Kurds are expected to just say, "Okay, come and kill us." If they defend themselves, it is seen as a problem, because nobody is supposed to raise a fist or an arm against the state as the sole holder of monopoly over violence.

This is, however, an issue for revolutionary movements as well. What kind of violence? Revolutionary violence has been talked about a lot. But in practice, and you can see this in the books *Roots of Civilization* and *The PKK and the Kurdish Question in the 21st Century* that you have to limit violence, because everyone has assimilated the approach of the state tradition and its practices, especially masculinity, the masculinity of it.[2] Öcalan calls the state the "institutionalized male." This is also why women and their entry into the struggle is so immensely important. Revolutionary violence was always on the agenda for critique and self-critique. There were moments where both forms of violence were becoming increasingly similar, and you had to tie that down. This is why I say that it is an immense dialectic of growing and developing, with no fear of putting yourself on the operating table. They didn't just critique everything else, including Marxism and Leninism, and everybody else; first and foremost, they critiqued themselves. And this is how the movement arrived at the concept of revolutionary violence uniquely defined as self-defense. Violence triggers hierarchy, whereas self-defense is grounded in social and political mechanisms, so as not to regenerate patriarchy, statehood, or statism. More on that later.

By the 1990s, there was a huge debate about and analysis of real socialism within the Kurdish freedom movement. The movement didn't arrive at this rupture very easily or very quickly. What they didn't do, and this is where I think Öcalan's role is very important, is that they didn't just scrap the idea. They didn't get rid of the idea of revolution, freedom, women's freedom, people's freedom, etc. Their own practice cast a light further back into the development and reorientation of the armed struggle, because they live in a specific part of the world. Let's not forget the recent threat in the form of ISIS, which did not begin as a force that targeted the Kurdish people for elimination, but in the hands of Turkish state, in particular, quickly became a massive fascist force that essentially tried to eliminate the Kurdish freedom movement's accumulations. This is why Öcalan calls the Middle East a "strategic battleground for World War III." And this is why the collapse of ISIS, the strategic loss of ISIS in Kobanî, was immensely important for all of humanity. We can already see that otherwise fascism would have been knocking on everybody's door much sooner. Even within the current limitations, we are seeing a substantial rollback of working-class and women's rights everywhere in the world. So, yes, it's all connected. Nothing is as separate from anything else as one might think at first.

Q: *You mentioned all the martyrs and the women and men and families that have been sacrificed, so thank you again for your bravery. My question is on the subject of the fascist conditions in the area that you mentioned, something that a lot of the people here are probably thinking about in relation to your talk. The issue of fear or hopelessness among the people and the conditions that you might see giving people hope to take on certain actions at great cost to themselves and their families, including cultural things that get passed on, like having a strong identity. A lot of people from different diasporas in the United States grow up far removed from that, but possibly we understand that we have a connection to our own culture and the armed struggle that occurred a couple of generations ago. However, the conditions here feel hopeless, because of the repression that exists, especially of Black and Brown people here. Maybe you could say a few words about that. Thank you.*

Havin: We didn't actually get to speak about what is happening presently, so I'm glad this question has come up, because it is, of course, immensely important to be able to put what is happening into perspective. As I said, Öcalan and the Kurdish freedom movement call this World War III, and it is, as you can see, in different stages of happening, especially in the Middle East, in a very physical sense. There is an overlap of several different hegemonic wars going on. On the one hand, global capital, especially that of the United States but also that of other imperialist entities, is trying to abrogate any rule or law. It wants complete access to the entire world. On the other hand, we have national capital, which is both in conflict and allied—as paradoxical as it may sound—to prevent that to a degree. Where they overlap is in their unrestricted desire to exploit and colonize. This is why Trump here and Erdoğan there and the right-wing gaining strength in Germany are basically one and the same.

ISIS can also be seen as exactly the same threat. And they are all about talking about male "suffering" or loss of power. Because what they are doing is trying to empower the male— I'm using this in a negative sense—so that he can become its paramilitary agent, its hand within society for reshaping society. ISIS is the most extreme form of that, but Erdoğan is doing the same thing. However, I don't want to personalize this. I don't want to say "Erdoğan" or "Trump," because everybody kind of thinks it's only Erdoğan or it's only Trump. We must see the institutional dimensions and aspects. It's not just some lunatic out there, and, whoever it may be, it is not an individual. To the contrary, it is very organized. The way they are analyzed or perceived is such that it disempowers us. If we see them as lunatics, we won't do much about it. We hope that one day the lunatic is taken to the hospital or dies or something, but, in the meantime, there are structural changes in our world. And they are making those changes together. At first, they tried to do it through proxies, like ISIS, al-Qaeda, and all the others. This didn't really work, and now they are really getting down to the nitty-gritty—the trade wars, the reversal of disarmament.

When we talk about global capital, we are talking not only about US capital but also about Chinese and Russian capital and others, including German capital. In the meantime, everybody is trying to expand their hegemony. But you know where I think the hopelessness comes from? It is the result of seeing ourselves as objects of this and not subjective agents who have also contributed to this structural crisis of capitalism. We also did this. It's not just transnational or global capital that brought about the structural crisis of capitalism. It's the women's movements, and, and no matter how profound our critique, it's the national liberation movements as well. It's all those who resisted and struggled. Again, it is colonized people, Black people, Kurdish people, all those at the bottom who were aggrieved by the capitalist system, who fought against it, as well as global capital at the top, that now sees these structures as an obstacle. So we almost have a situation where global capital is overlapping with what the oppressed are doing. It's interesting. This is why some people get confused about what the Kurds are doing in the Middle East. Because some want to see the Kurds as on the side of the US or Russia or some imperialist power like that. While others argue that the Kurds should just accept the old status quo. There are two very different ideological ends that are destroying this status quo. On the one hand, global capital, because the status quo is an obstacle, and, on the other hand, the revolutionary movements. Of course, we must be careful. These alliances and networks must be forged very thoughtfully, and this situation cannot be seen as hopeless but as an option for transition.

This is where the media is being used extremely well by capital, so that we don't see this moment of creative and artistic freedom. Look at it. Look at the amount of violence. It is almost pornographic. They show us ISIS beheadings, and even cats being raped, and all the oppression and the violence that is going on—the recolonization of people everywhere. They are hoping that the oppressed and the colonized do not seize the moment. And when I say seize the moment, I don't mean it in the old way, you know, "Let's bring down the state." No. This has been done. It has been done in the Soviet Union and elsewhere. Let's save these discussions for tomorrow and the next day. If seizing the moment does not mean taking over the state, then what does it mean? Kurds, women, and others in Syria, in Rojava, are showing us what that might be.

However you look at it, you must acknowledge that if the Kurdish freedom movement did not act in the way it did in Syria, today's Syria would have been another Libya, because the hegemonic powers do not want stability. They have no need for stability. Do we not remember what happened in Libya? Does nobody remember? Is there an actual government there now? What's happening there? Nobody wants stability. Let's not be fooled. Today, peace denotes surrender. Don't do anything. Acceptance, submission, that is what peace is. This is the way it's being used. Therefore, I love the way Öcalan describes what is happening. He says, "I call this age, the Age of Hope." We know so much more than we previously knew—in terms of history, in terms of women's enslavement, in terms of colonization, in terms of the formation of classes throughout time. However, there is a need to organize and establish peoples' social and political systems in a way that allows us to come out of this World War III, to benefit everyone who is struggling for freedom. Therefore, this is the Age of Hope, but it won't happen on its own, and we are beginning to see that.

As I said, this moment is being used by organized gangs in different places throughout the world to increase the level of fascism. They are both creating displaced people and using this influx of migration to recolonize the people of the West, by producing propaganda that claims migrants will lower wages, undermine the Western way of life, and so on. The way things can be twisted to again benefit the establishment of that system is savagery. We say, "Why say no to migrants? Say no to colonization and the war that creates the refugees and migrants."

This gets lost in the volume of what they dish out to us and the speed with which they do it. It's so fast; everything is so fast. And again, it's a form of consumption. Everything and everyone is very quickly consumed. Therefore, we can live with it, but it's not a life. Otherwise, how is it that we are okay with people disappearing in the middle of the sea? How can we justify this by saying, "I will have less bread if you come"? It's not even clear that that is true. In the crisis in Turkey, as is the case with the real estate crisis here, it's not the banks, it's not this and that who are losing. It's not the Turkish state or the government that is losing either. It's the people who are losing. But it is portrayed so differently that, in Europe, there is, as a result, once again a call for people to embrace their states, which goes hand in hand with a call for men to be in charge and become more sexist, and nationalist, etc.

The thing is, there is so much to be hopeful about. You know why? Despite what's happening in Turkey, people are resisting. It may be quiet, but there is resistance. You saw what happened in the elections. Despite all the oppression, bloodbaths, stealing of votes, etc., Adalet ve Kalkınma Partisi (Justice and Development Party; AKP) couldn't get over that 50 percent mark. There is huge resistance everywhere, and I think that we do it a grave injustice if we only look at what's happening in the world as the scheme of imperialism alone. Those struggling for freedom have to see their part in this and act accordingly.

And we must do so together. We can't just say, "Ah, great, look at what's happening in Rojava." It's possible everywhere. What is important is not to fall into protecting the status quo. I remember watching the elections between Trump and Hillary from afar. Gosh, you would have thought Hillary was a revolutionary. And everybody was called on to vote for her. This is what is happening in Turkey. In Turkey, against Erdoğan, everybody, even the European states, of course, is pointing to the Cumhuriyet Halk Partisi (Republican People's Party; CHP), calling it *the* opposition. But it can only truly be oppositional if it overcomes itself. The status quo is no longer sustainable. Thus, they are trying to show that this is a fight between the old status quo and that of this new situation whatever it's going to be, because it's still unclear what this new thing will become.

This is what the freedom movement means by a third way. They are saying, "No, we don't want the status quo, neither the old nor the new status quo." And it's not just the Kurds who don't want what has been the status quo in the Middle East. It's just more apparent in the case of Kurdish people, because there was simply no room for their existence within the old status quo. We are like the Blacks of the Middle East. There was just no room for us. The left thought the freedom movement was nationalist. The right thought it was made up of atheists and lunatics. Stalinists, whatever. There was just no room. This may have made it easier to understand the whole thing. But it is really difficult for those who think they have privileges to figure it out. I think it's a little more difficult to crack for those who have a state. I mean, is the state really theirs? A s the Kurds showed in Syria, "No, we are not with Assad, but we are not necessarily against him as an individual. Institutionally, this regime was not just bad for the Kurds; it was not good for anyone. And, no, we are not with the imperialists; we have principles—freedom for women, no exploitation, no colonization, no abuse, no stealing of the surplus product in the form of taxes, interest rates, or otherwise."

This is why we call it the third way. For a long time, until ISIS came along, everybody ignored the Kurdish freedom movement or, worse, criminalized it. "Who are they? Are they with Assad? Are they with the US? Are they with. . .? No they are with Russia." Of course, some mistakes might have been made, but the truth of the matter is that the freedom movement in Rojava just tried to steer clear of it all, to just rebuild, create, and defend itself, to do something different. And this is why this moment is as comprehensive, even more so, than the moment just before World War I. It is that comprehensive. And it is that historic. This is why it is the Age of Hope.

Q: *When you were speaking about bringing the critique to people, what exactly did that look like? Were there materials? How did you bring this critique of states and their ideologies to the people? Were there pamphlets? How did this look?*

Havin: As I said, in the next couple of days, we will delve more deeply into this. Yes, there are texts, but the most important way is oral, by consistently talking with people. I have to say that it was, of course, a very difficult process. In fact, Öcalan called this his third birth. He said his first birth was from his mother, the natural birth. His second birth was the founding of the PKK, because this meant a rupture with the Turkish state ideology and reenvisioning a contemporary Kurdish identity. The concept of Kurdishness has also evolved quite a bit. It's not as simple as ethnicity anymore. And I will talk about that in terms of democratic nation as well on the last day. This is not about the Kurdish nation becoming democratic. Keep all of that in mind for later. The third birth was this new paradigm, especially the rupture with the state itself.

The fact is that births are extremely painful. In the case of a woman giving birth, we are told that if a man did it he would probably die, because the pain is so extreme. Öcalan's choice of words can help us to possibly understand to some degree how difficult this was, this severing, this breaking away—both from masculinity and from the idea of the state. This process is continuing. If we were to say that all is good and well, that it's done with, that would not be true. No.

I recall a big protest meeting in Europe in the early days of this discussion about breaking away from the idea of a state. At first, of course, people thought that Öcalan was being tactical. "It's tactics." A lot of people wanted to believe that, instead of trying to understand what he was getting at. But, at the same time, due to all the years of struggle, they trusted him. As I said, it's a tested relationship. They were prepared to open their minds and ears to understand why he was saying what he was saying. I remember in one meeting somebody was giving a speech at the gathering and said, "What do you want? Freedom or the state?" And people responded, "The state!" (laughing) The speaker said, "Come on, what do you want? Freedom?" And people replied, "Yeah, okay, freedom." This process is still going on, of course. It may not be the case anymore, for example, but maybe fifty years ago, children who were born without fathers would be called bastards and would not be accepted in society. Peoples without a state in this world are in a similar situation. The world order is one of nations with states. It meant that you would have nowhere to go. If you were the victims of genocide, where would you go? You can't go to the United Nations, because it's United Nation-States. It's not the United Nations. If you have a state, you can go there. You can't go to the International Court of Justice in Netherlands, because, again, only states can take their issues there, or you need a state ready to take on your case. Who would do that? They are partners in crime or entangled in economic and political interests and profits. Where do you go? There is nowhere for you to go. And, therefore, peoples without a state thought having a state facilitated freedom. But then we see all these other peoples with a state, and we see they too are not free, but they may have some privileges over others. There are lots of different borders drawn and seeming privileges created, although it is all relative. It's all relative.

This process is continuing. These discussions are continuing. And in the case of Rojava, people in Northern Kurdistan, and even more so in Southern Kurdistan, are seeing how this ideology, this paradigm, is so much more suitable. The Kurdistan regional government in Southern Kurdistan is already a very primitive state—a pre-state. We are seeing that a victim can very quickly become a perpetrator. It's not about your ethnicity. It's not about this or that. It's about this tool of statehood. This tool itself is oppressive. It barbaric. It's an organized mafia. We see it in the form of the Israeli state. They were first victims, and now they are perpetrators. We are seeing it in South Africa. We are seeing how the tool of state is corrupting what was once a freedom movement. We saw it in the Soviet Union. When it collapsed, all the worst things came out of it: sexism, nationalism, religionism. They all burst out of it. People have embraced this new paradigm, but in the finer details there is still a lot of headway to be made. This is simply how it is. The notion of an overnight revolution was wrong. Some things can occur overnight, but to get rid of the characteristics or traits that have been created in each one of us requires a lot of struggle. This is what is called simultaneous critique and self-critique. Each individual has to fight with themselves as well. We have all been educated in a particular way for a long time—and we still are. If we are not at school, we are watching a film. If we are not watching a film, we are watching the news. If we are not watching the news, we are on Twitter. If we are not on Twitter… There is continuous regeneration. We have to combat that somehow, which requires insistent and continuous mechanisms. But, mostly, it requires a willingness, a desire, to rid ourselves of all of this.

This opens whole new horizons of freedom and whole new horizons of joy. We often hear the term *burning out*. What burning out? Is this a burden? This is not a burden. This is our life! Waging struggle must bring joy. You know how that is done? If you develop as an individual while you struggle, you won't burn out. If you think you are doing it for somebody else, that actually you're so good that you're freeing somebody else, then, yeah, burning out is a possibility. Definitely.

Notes

1   A concept also coined by Abdullah Öcalan; see Abdullah Öcalan, *The Sociology of Freedom: Manifesto of the Democratic Civilization*, vol. 3 (Oakland: PM Press, 2020).

2   Abdullah Öcalan, *Prison Writings I: The Roots of Civilization* (London: Pluto Press, 2007); Abdullah Öcalan, *Prison Writings II: The PKK and Kurdish Question in the 21st Century* (London: Pluto Press, 2011).

The Rebellion of the Oldest Colony—*Jineolojî*, the Science of Women and Life

We discussed the freedom movement's evaluation process a little yesterday, but it's important to understand where the need for evaluation came from and at exactly what point this reevaluation occurred. The Kurdish freedom movement is part of a stream of freedom and equality struggles, part of a chain of struggles that stretches back through five thousand years of patriarchy. The PKK, the Kurdish freedom struggle and movement, sees itself as the sum of all these struggles and resistances. What it has done through its lifetime has been to try to learn from these struggles and to deduce results from the evaluation of its own praxis and implementation. It has turned those lessons into new ideas and new tools. The underlying reason for that is that nothing is ever taken at face value. At a time when most of the Marxist-Leninist movements, not just in the Middle East but around the world, were basing themselves around the axis of one country or another, like Albania or China or the Soviet Union, the PKK didn't actually do this. Although it was established as a Marxist-Leninist organization, it wasn't dependent per se on one implementation or another. What it began to question in late 1980s, but especially after the collapse of the Soviet Union, as well as with the standstill of feminism, was: Why? What happened? What happened that despite their sincerity, the sincerity of the 1968 movements, the national liberation movements, the October Revolution, they all ended up in the same place? Instead of losing hope—we talked about hope and imagination a lot yesterday—what the PKK began to do was to question. Simultaneous to this questioning process, the organization tried to take precautions so that similar mistakes would not be repeated.

At this point, the structural crisis of capitalism is more visible, and given that we are going through World War III, there are new interventions into the Middle East. One of the new interventions, as I mentioned yesterday, was to force Öcalan out of Syria in 1998. When they didn't get what they wanted from that, it was the invasion of Afghanistan and Iraq. It has been happening continuously. In fact, what we are seeing all around the world—they tried this with the Kurdish freedom movement too—is an attempt to eliminate all organized movements, so that they are not obstacles to whatever is going to develop instead of capitalism, and it is still not clear what will develop instead of capitalism. The situation we have now is the collapse of the order that was constructed in the aftermath of the two world wars.

This is not only the result of an imperial project; it is also a result of our struggles. At this point, what the hegemonic powers, or the rulers, whether domestic or global capital, are trying to do is to make sure individuals are not in a position to resist or build something new, that they are not organized. Therefore, even smaller organizations, like the zone à défendre (zones to defend; ZAD) in France—all they are doing is living collectively in a rural area and working the land collectively, and they are organized in that sense—even organizations like that are not tolerated. Or we could look at the Fuerzas Armadas Revolucionarias de Colombia (Revolutionary Armed Forces of Colombia; FARC), for example. It shows us another way of assimilating and eliminating an organized force. Whether or not we agree with the FARC's ideology, what we are seeing is that its inclusion in the political system—without the state keeping its promises—has cleared the way for a huge pillaging of resources, and its sympathizers are being killed by paramilitary forces. So there is a colonization, a recolonization process by the state, that is going on in that case. We talked about the Tamil people too and how their genocide went unnoticed by the world. The Turkish state tried something similar with the Kurds in the aftermath of the collapse of the talks in 2014.

Let's go back a bit to the presence of women among the founding members of the PKK and later as part of the resistance and struggle of PKK members in general and in the notorious Diyarbakır prison. The resistance of women, particularly that of the founding member of the PKK Sakine Cansız, soon became almost mythical. The Kurdish people's aspirations for freedom, especially that of Kurdish women, and, as I just said, more specifically Sakine Cansız's relentless struggle and resistance in the face of the horrendous torture she was subjected to, paved the way for women to play a huge role. Sakine Cansız, I should add, was later assassinated, along with two other revolutionaries, in Paris, on January 9, 2013, just after the beginning of talks between the Turkish state and Öcalan and the PKK.

In the beginning, the women's struggle within the PKK did not go beyond the borders of the old left, but it could not be contained by it either. Öcalan's role, both as a strategist and as the political leader of the Kurdish freedom movement, is important here. He did not ignore the enslavement of women or their desires and their struggle for freedom. Despite negative reactions from some male members of the organization, he opened political, social, cultural, ideological, and organizational space for women and stood strongly behind this.

Women joined the guerrilla forces from the beginning because of the sexism they faced within the feudal tribal structures, as well as the fury they felt in the face of increasing colonialist and exploitative oppression of the Kurds at the hands of the Turkish state. People from all walks of life came together to wage a common struggle. The very first problem

was encountered immediately. Joining a revolutionary movement was not enough on its own to overcome the patriarchal
and other characteristics drawn from the colonialist and
feudal structures. Problems began to emerge especially in the
approach to women; there was an attempt at regenerating traditional roles among the guerrilla forces and within the party
structures. Remember that we said that they didn't just critique
the different freedom struggles or feminism or whatever; they
also looked at their own practice. And, of course, in doing so,
they saw all of this very, very clearly. Women were present in
the beginning, during the foundation of the movement, but as
the movement entered the armed struggle phase, and as the participation of women began to increase, this question imposed
itself more forcefully on the movement's agenda. What they
saw was that there was something close to a replication of the
old gender roles. Women waged a huge struggle within the
movement. Although it was a revolutionary movement, they
were facing a more or less similar situation. For example, one
issue that arose was that after the mid-1980s, toward the end of
the 1980s, some of the commanders were sending the women
back to the cities, because the mountains "were just too difficult for them." The attitude that developed by some toward
the women who came to the mountains was: "They should just
do cooking and wait. Prepare the ammunition." What was
really important within this movement was the presence of
one of the founding leaders of the Kurdish freedom movement,
Abdullah Öcalan, who did not turn a blind eye to this problem,
and this is why the women in the movement call Öcalan the
most radical comrade, the most revolutionary comrade. As a
leader of the movement, he didn't turn a blind eye and say, "This
is not something that concerns us." It's so much easier to just
have the movement adopt very general principles. Instead, he
made sure that they did not just resist and rebel as individuals,
but that they did so in an organized manner. Organizationally,
theoretically, and politically he supported and paved the way.

There were women who accepted the replication of these roles, and there were women who rejected it. Thus, the organization quickly realized the severity of the problem and, in 1987, established the Yekîtiya Jinên Welatparêzên Kurdistan (Union of Patriotic Women of Kurdistan; YJWK). The foundation of this union was the very first declaration of the intention to establish an autonomous and separate women's organization.

The huge influx of women in the 1990s compelled the formation of a new organization within the guerrilla forces. In 1993, for the very first time, autonomous women's units were formed. This meant that they would not be under the direct command of the male guerrillas and would be able to make their own decisions and plans and determine how to implement those plans. The subsequent development of women's role in self-defense increased women's self-confidence, leading to enormous ideological, political, and social transformations. This was a second breakthrough, following the heroic resistance of women in Turkish prisons. Indeed, it led to revolutionary changes in how women were perceived by men and within the Kurdish society in general.

In 1995, the Yekitiya Azadîya Jinên Kurdistan (Free Women's Association of Kurdistan; YAJK) was formed. From then on, political and societal work was not only taken up by the women in the organization but by society at large. At the same time, international solidarity work began. It was during these years that Öcalan began talking about a new concept: *killing the [dominant] male*. Therefore, in this context, it is very important to problematize the question of the male—not only the question women's freedom but of men's freedom as well. Why are men not transforming themselves, or even seeing the need to do so? This is why the fundamental principle of democratic socialism inside the Kurdish freedom movement is referred to as *killing the [dominant] male*. What we are seeing is that there are so many instances of privilege enjoyed by different agents: men over women, white over Black, mother over children, etc.—and in terms of nations as well. For example, the Turkish state's oppression of the Kurds is also entrapping Turkish society and preventing it from becoming more democratic. What we need to understand, and this is perhaps one of the ways in which both Öcalan and the Kurdish freedom movement are able to convince the Kurdish society and the male revolutionaries as well, is that the enslavement of women is not just about women. It is not just about biology. Men's freedom is lost as well. All of this has to do with stealing the surplus product, and it begins with the women, because the order that protected surplus product from theft was the result of the morals that were instilled during the matriarchal age.

From 1995 on, the women's freedom struggle became more radicalized. In 1992, in discussion with the women, Öcalan said, "If you don't find a solution to men's mentality, then all of your lives are in danger." And, later, he introduced the concept of *killing the [dominant] man*. People usually think that this is an evaluation that postdates 1999, but it's from 1996. I am told that actually most men were a bit scared [jokingly]. They said, "Hey, this is not literal, right? You're not going to kill us with a gun or something?" No, of course not. The theory behind this development became very far-reaching. There was a talk of eternal divorce, for example. This eternal divorce wasn't just meant for women. It also was meant for men. It referred to divorcing the five-thousand-year-old patriarchal political and social system and its mindset, both psychologically and culturally. At the same time, they talked about a parallel project to transform men. To this end, women took over educating men.

As 1998 approached, the women laid down the principles of the ideology of women's liberation, and to implement them they formed the Partiya Jinên Karkerên Kurdistan (Women Workers' Party of Kurdistan; PJKK). In 2000, the women broadened their perspective on organization and struggle and founded the Partiya Jina Azad (Party of the Free Woman; PJA).

One of the most important achievements of this era was the declaration of a Women's Social Contract.

However, all these attempts did not totally overcome the limits and framework of patriarchy. Not only the women's movement but the whole organization was searching for an alternative. Although the PKK was no longer the old left, it was nonetheless unable to come up with a solution that completely broke away from real socialism, and, with it, capitalist modernity. One can define the period from 1993 to 2003 as the transition period, accompanied by the attempt to establish an alternative to capitalist modernity. The available theoretical material, the past experiences of various other movements and of feminism, and the very experience of the PKK led Öcalan and the movement to conclude that women's enslavement constituted the very basis of all subsequent enslavement, as well as all other social problems. Thus, it began to distinguish itself from classic Marxism-Leninism. It also differed in the way it began to view the state apparatus as an instrument of power and exploitation that is unnecessary for the continuation of human and natural life. Finally, its perception of revolutionary violence also changed, with it being framed as self-defense.

Öcalan determined that women's slavery had been perpetuated on three levels over five thousand years. First, there was the construction of ideological slavery, then the use of force, and, finally, the economy was seized from her. He was quick to make the connection between the depth of women's enslavement, the intentional masking of this fact, and the rise of hierarchical and statist power within society. As women were habituated to slavery, the path to the enslavement of the other sections of society was paved. The enslavement of men follows the enslavement of women. However, women's enslavement is different in some ways to class and nation enslavement. It is legitimized by refined and intense repression combined with lies that play on emotions. Women's biological difference from men is used to justify her enslavement. All the work she does is taken for granted and treated as the *unworthy work of women.*

Without analyzing the process by which women were socially overcome, you can neither understand the fundamental characteristics of the existent male-dominated social culture or what to build in its place. Without understanding how masculinity was socially formed, you cannot analyze the institution of state and, therefore, will not be able to accurately define the culture of war and power related to statehood. This is something we need to emphasize, because this is what paved the way for femicide and the colonization and exploitation of peoples. The social subjugation of women was the vilest counterrevolution ever carried out. Öcalan points out that "the sword of war wielded by the state and by the hand of the man within the family are symbols of hegemony. The entire classed society, from its upper to its lower layers, is caught between the sword and the hand."

Öcalan goes back to history and interprets not only the written facts but the mythologies as well, in order to be able to understand where the truth lies when it comes to the loss of freedom—not only of women but of men and society as well.

The third very important thing was the seizure of the economy. In ancient Greek, *oikonomia,* is, of course, *householding* or *management of the home,* very much belittled nowadays, as if householding is petty or something. The seizure of the economy: that of women and of peoples and so forth is also an important factor in the creation of this slavery. In fact, if you look at it, this conclusion makes it clear that all colonization, exploitation, and class formation fits this template. If you look at colonized peoples, you will see something very similar. I see how the Kurds were colonized and lost their freedom. It was done in exactly this way. First, there was an ideological construct that sparked and imposed auto-assimilation, a process in which you are told, "You are the other. You're not human." To counter that you try to take on your oppressor's identity.

My father used to tell us that when he went to primary school, he didn't know any Turkish. At school, the children would tease him and others like him, saying, "Kurds have tails." They would ask, "Where is your tail? You have a tail. Where is it?" My father would go home crying and ask his mother, "Mom, where's my tail?" Or they would say Kurds were dirty or smelly or incestuous or not so bright. I think this is not just the case for the Kurds but for any group of people who are discriminated against. It's a way to ensure that the target people abandon their identity and begin to auto-assimilate.

Of course, for those who do not embrace this ideological construct and are not convinced by the sheer violence and psychological effect it has, there is violence proper—physical violence. Just as was the case with us, women. Women were burned. They were buried alive for centuries. They were beaten so badly that all their bones were broken. In some of the ancient traditions, women's feet are still bound in very tight footwear or in iron shoes, so that they can't walk very fast. This was imposed as something to be *seen* as symbol of beauty, when, in fact, it was a symbol of domination. And if this does not suffice, women are stripped of their livelihoods. It is not only the economy of women that is seized but also that of colonized peoples and of workers overall. This, for example, is the case for the Kurds. All of their resources, including any control over their day-to-day economic activities, has been taken away from them. This is the case in capitalist countries as well. Communities and peoples have their economies seized to make them dependent on the system—on a wage or on welfare.

Analytically, capitalism and the nation-state are seen as representing the dominant male in the most institutionalized form. Capitalist society is the continuation and culmination of all the previous exploitative societies. It is, in fact, a continuous war against society and women. To put it simply, capitalism and the nation-state are the monopoly of the tyrannical and exploitative male. It is enough to look around the world to see a renewed increase in the violence and exploitation, and the renewed suppression of women. This is not happening only in so-called Third World countries but all over the world.

A main objective of capitalist modernity's ideological hegemony is to obliterate and obscure the historic and social facts concerning its conception and its essence. The capitalist economic and societal form is not a historical or societal necessity; it is a construct, forged in a complex process. Religion and philosophy have been transformed into nationalism: the divinity of the nation-state. The ultimate goal of its ideological warfare is to ensure its monopoly on thought. Its main weapons to accomplish this are religionism, gender discrimination, and scientism as positivist religion. Maintaining modernity without ideological hegemony, with political and military oppression alone, would be impossible. Öcalan was quick to make the point that while capitalism uses religionism to control society's cognizance, it uses nationalism to control classes and citizens, a phenomenon that arose with capitalism. The objective of gender discrimination is to deny women any hope of change. Öcalan says the most effective way for sexist ideology to function is by entrapping men in power relations and rendering women impotent through constant rape. Through positivist scientism, capitalism neutralizes the academic world and the youth. It convinces them that they have *no choice* but to integrate into the system, and that this integration will secure them concessions.

Clarifying the status of women is only one aspect of this issue. The question of liberation is far more important. In other words, resolving the problem is more import than just revealing and analyzing it. During the last quarter of the twentieth century, feminism managed to disclose the truth about women to a certain extent, which was very important for all of us. But the Kurdish women's freedom movement and Abdullah Öcalan take a step further and base their analysis of society on "moral and political society." They draw a relationship between freedom and morality and freedom and politics. To develop structures that expand our area of freedom, morality is defined as the collective conscience of society and politics as its shared wisdom. How do we now work toward this?

Thus, the women's freedom movement went through several periods of restructuring. There was a need for a women's organization that transcended party structures, a more flexible and comprehensive confederal women's organization. In 2005, the Koma Jinên Bilind (High Council of Women; KJB) was founded. As a result, there was organizational and practical restructuring to implement the new paradigm based on democracy, ecology, and women's freedom. The KJB was established as the coordination point between the self-defense forces, social organizations, the women's party, or PAJK, and young women's organizations. In September 2014, the organization of women went through another transformation and has, in the meantime, changed its name accordingly to the Komalên Jinên Kurdistan (Kurdistan Women's Community; KJK). This transformation was needed to equally and comprehensively deal with the needs of society and the formation of required institutions, in order to continue with the transformation of men, the democratization of society, and the creation of the ethics and aesthetics of free life but most importantly and in parallel redefining who they are as woman. As such, women are organizing themselves both at the local level and in all decision-making structures. They make all decisions that concern them on their own and take their place at the local level and at all the different levels where decisions that concern the whole society are made. Other sections of society—the youth, the elderly, professions, belief systems, craftworkers—are also organized so that power and hierarchic formations and structures cannot be perpetuated, with mechanisms in place to ensure that they don't arise.

If women's slavery was perpetuated on three levels: the construction of ideological slavery, the use of force, and the seizure of the economy from her, then these three areas must addressed, and she must also organize simultaneously herself to counter them.

Öcalan's main thesis is that before patriarchy and state civilization there was another system in which the position of women in society was very different. Indeed, society was matriarchal and had very different principles for sustaining itself, namely, sharing and solidarity. Now, this "democratic civilization," as he calls it, has not disappeared but continues to exist. However, it is constantly being exploited and its area narrowed by patriarchal state civilization. Öcalan sees the historical struggle of the last five thousand years as a struggle between state civilization and democratic civilization, the latter consisting of pre-state nomadic village and agricultural communities.

We can see that the loss of freedom is simultaneously the history of how women lost their position and vanished from history. The fierce struggle between matriarchy and patriarchy can also be seen throughout Sumerian mythology from 4000 BCE onward. Later, in the Babylonian creation myth, we see the end of this process, when the goddess Tiamat is killed by her son Marduk—the god of war. In fact, we see that women's downfall and loss is the downfall and loss of the whole society. The result is sexist society, with dominant male gaining power, culminating in patriarchy. Öcalan reached the conclusion that all other forms of slavery have been developed on the basis of women's enslavement. Thus, if women's enslavement is not overcome no other form of enslavement can be overcome, not only because all enslavement mimics women's enslavement but also because they are all built upon it.

The fierce struggle we are talking about is not one between the sexes, although it has turned into that too as a result of shaping men and women to this end, but is about the principles of social order. Originally, the term hierarchy referred to government by the priests and the authority of the wise elders.

Initially, along with women, the wise elders played a positive role in a society that was not based on accumulation and ownership. They ensured communal security and the governance of society. But when voluntary dependence is transformed into authority and usefulness into self-interest, it gives way to the instrument of force, disguised as security for all and collective production. This constitutes the core of all exploitative and oppressive systems. The overcoming of the matriarchal order had strategic significance; without it, patriarchy and the accompanying statist power would not have been victorious. To institutionalize this, women's biological difference from men was used to justify her enslavement. The institutionalization of this ideological construct of women was gradual and resulted in her becoming the common slave of both the ordinary enslaved man in the home and the dominant man who was institutionalized as the state.

A hierarchical and authoritarian structure is essential for a patriarchal society. The establishment of patriarchal relations, on the other hand, is a fundamental stage on the path to class division and state formation. Therefore, we must understand these relations profoundly, because neither the state nor the class society structures it is based upon can be explained if the status of women is not analyzed thoroughly. To be able to understand the fundamental characteristics of the male-dominated society's culture, we need not only to understand how women were socially defeated but how constraint and dependency was established over the youth as well. This is another aspect of patriarchy attaining its strength. The physical strength of the youth is needed. Such constructed dependency continues today and cannot easily be smashed. Youth, like womanhood, is not only a physical phenomenon but also a social construct. Öcalan argues that the strategy used against women, including the tactics, the ideological and political propaganda, and the oppressive systems, has also been used against the youth. This is why the youth desire freedom, not only because they are young but because of the unique social oppression they are subjected to but are not yet habituated to.

From this, it follows that if we do not understand how the male was socially constructed we cannot correctly analyze the state institution or, therefore, the "war" and "power" culture that comes with the state.

Hierarchical society is seen as the link between natural society and statist society based on class. At the beginning, authority is personal. However, the institutionalization of authority amounts to a qualitative transformation. The state is essentially the authority that has gained permanence and been institutionalized since the Sumerians, and it is not just any authority; it is military and political authority.

So what is power? Öcalan defines power as the state of execution of the state institution. It is the activity of seizing the surplus values and the product of women and society. Why is it so attractive? Because to be in power is to own the accumulated riches and the institutions and to control the rules, as well as the force and methods, necessary for continued expansion. Thus, Öcalan reaches the conclusion that you cannot make a revolution or effect a transformation by attaining power. The only thing that you can do with power is seize values and redistribute them.

But where does power draw its strength from? This question and others like it lead us to the source of power, which is might, and might is determined in war. Thus, the source of the state and hence of power is not societal intelligence but might and war. As such, the state and power are not formed as the instruments for resolving societal problems. On the contrary, they are the source of societal problems. The phenomenon of war that the state has rested upon since coming into existence continues. War is the foundation of power. To be in power is to mold every dimension of a society and to maintain a certain status quo on the basis of the culture of war.

It has taken a while to truly understand that the tool that has been propagated as a magic wand—the state—has always been an instrument that creates class division and inequalities and, most importantly, legalizes and legitimizes the seizure of surplus product and values—including and especially those of women. Öcalan has come to the conclusion that the state as an apparatus cannot be an instrument for achieving freedom. On the contrary, it is an obstacle to being free. Thus, there is a revolutionary paradigm shift in the analysis of the enslavement of women and nature and, therefore, of society.

For the Kurdish freedom movements, these insights have led to a number of conclusions:

1) Do not interpret a people's right to self-determination as requiring the acquisition of a nation-state. The proposal of democratic confederalism is not an alternative state but an alternative to the state.

2) Do not act in a state- and power-centered way but wage a struggle that is centered on democracy, women's freedom, and an ecological society and that strives to construct an alternative life on that basis.

3) Develop an ideology based on moral and political society that is grounded in solidarity.

4) Interpret history through this lens and write a true history of women.

5) Develop the ability to differentiate between self-defense and violence or force on the basis of whether or not it is revolutionary.

6) Do not base the economy on accumulation of surplus values and products but on society's collective needs-based decisions.

7) Make knowledge available to all in order to prevent the creation of monopoly over knowledge.

To this end all the sections of society that have been traditionally exploited and suppressed should have independent organizations. This applies above all to women and the youth, but it should also include different peoples and groups that have been excluded from all decision-making structures and exploited and oppressed. This would allow those who have traditionally been excluded from decision-making structures to participate in overlapping structures, facilitating the creation of an internal dynamic for fighting against the reestablishment of patriarchy and its institutions at every moment of every day. Those traditionally excluded will not be acting as individuals but as the representatives—the collective being—of autonomous movements and organizations, which will give them leverage in whatever structure they find themselves, given that although they are there as an individual they represent an organized group, for example, women in a mixed council, commune or municipality, political party, and the like. This, in turn, will allow representatives to avoid power-centered conflicts and hold the interests of those they represent at the heart of their struggle.

Self-defense is central in this regard. The inequality that has been constructed between states and peoples is replicated between men and women. Therefore, self-defense is not just about physical defense but also about building independent structures for women to defend themselves from a range of inequality—from repression inside the family and educational system to the violence of the state. This has a revolutionizing effect on society, and this is also what is behind Turkish state's vicious attack on the women and the youth. They hope the use of extraordinary violence will stop women and the youth from seizing the opportunity to expand freedom for all.

Öcalan insistently examined this history in search of answers, especially as regards the state. If somebody asked me what really changed after 1999, I would say that he clearly broke with the idea of the state, which put everything else in sharper clarity and made it easier to interpret what happened and why, including why so many different struggles tended to end up at much the same point over time. He concluded that women's enslavement is not a result but the source of slavery itself. Using this approach, he also engaged in an anthropology of religion, of hierarchy, of power and might, and, as I have said, of the state. I have a friend who lives in Vermont, and he has a bookshop, used and new. He said, "When I got these books and read them, I initially put them in the history section. Then the next day, I thought, 'They don't belong there.' I moved them to social sciences, but then I thought 'They don't belong there either.' Then to philosophy," Finally, he thought, "Okay, they are just going to stay here on their own." That is because Abdullah Öcalan and the Kurdish freedom movement are not just intellectuals. They are not studying history for the sake of it. Nor are they operating only from women's point of view or a class point of view or a people's point of view. It's all more integral—more of a whole cloth. This is why Öcalan's books cannot be categorized under one heading alone, they are as holistic as life itself—because the idea is to not only to problematize capitalism and patriarchy in general but also to find a way to surpass them. Therefore, along with everything else, there is a huge responsibility to formulate a new way of living and what life is. In the midst of all of this questioning, there is also a far-reaching responsibility toward the Kurdish people. The early days were very, very critical, and this, of course, continues to be the case today. Öcalan subtitled his most recent book, volume 5, loosely translated, "*In the Grip of Genocide*," because it is at times like this that genocides occur, and Kurds have been in the grip of genocide for almost a century. But it is not all bleak. It is also an important opportunity unlike any previously in history. Well, perhaps there was a brief period immediately before World War I when a similar opportunity emerged for the oppressed. As such, I think the key issue over the last forty-five years, and even more so over the last twenty-five or so years, has been a constant requestioning and rethinking of everything.

Obviously, it is not enough to define the problem; we must also determine how we are going to rid ourselves of all of this. Of course, part of the problem lies in how the issues are defined. What the women's freedom movement and the freedom movement in general have done is to look at history through the lens of women's enslavement over time. From this point of view, the Neolithic era is seen as a period of women's revolution, but we see that there is no exaltation of women. The process is not viewed as essentialist. Women are not seen as superior because of their biological attributes or anything of that sort. The issue at hand is women's order or morality or way of life—the way that they led society during and before the Neolithic Age. It was this order of things and the accompanying mindset that were attacked and overthrown.

The first great sexual rupture is seen in the institutionalization of patriarchal authority and slavery in the form of housewifization, for which Öcalan sees three bases: ideology, violence, and the seizure of economy. This first great sexual rupture, which begins with the Sumerians because of the monopoly over surplus product, was necessary for the onset of patriarchal civilization. We can see that this new setup developed specifically because of the surplus product accumulated during the Neolithic era. The monopoly over the surplus product brings the need to establish control, and that brings with it authority. Before state structures could be formed, hierarchy necessarily had to emerge. This is a very important point. The second great sexual rupture occurs with feudalism—religions, feudalism, and the capitalist era. The patriarchal order claimed the first great sexual rupture as a cultural necessity arising from the production of substantial surplus product. During the second great sexual rupture, with the particular role of monotheistic religions, slavery and the deepening of enslavement of women are presented as God's will. As a result, Öcalan is adamant that victory in the third great sexual rupture must be won against the hegemonic male.

Of course, for all of this to happen, women had to be oversexualized, with their sexuality demonized. What is being argued is that capitalism and its nation-state represent the most highly institutionalized form of male hegemony. It is simultaneously the continuation and the peak of all colonial systems. Thus, it represents continuous warfare against society and women over time. Religionism, sexism, and scientism are the tools that enable it to do this. Currently, there is also a resurgence of this—a resurgence of both sexism and nationalism and the call on the male and the provocation for the socially constructed desire to dominate in the male to instill fascism. The positivist sciences render the academic world and the youth ineffective. In fact, *jineolojî* views the youth in a similar way; youth itself is also not a biological identity. It is precisely because of this oppression, the need to build or construct the youth in a certain way, that there is a youth rebellion much like that of women.

Both jineolojî and the sociology of freedom view the history of humanity in a novel way. One could say that the soul of the sociology of freedom is jineolojî. The middle class views history from point of view of the state, especially the nation-state: that is, from the perspective of the rise and fall of states. Marxism approaches the issue with a focus on class and economy. Öcalan's starting point is moral and political society, with women as its fulcrum. Therefore, he was able to develop a different definitional framework. He calls it democratic civilization, based on looking at what has happened to moral and political society over time. In doing so, he unifies the stories of all the oppressed and colonized who have been left out of this patriarchal and classical civilization, referring to them collectively as democratic civilization. Its form today is democratic modernity in opposition to capitalist modernity. This approach also establishes a relationship with freedom. This is a topic we will explore in greater detail to explain why Öcalan and the freedom movement base their paradigm on moral and political society.

Of course, jineolojî is not just about women, as *jin* in Kurdish means *woman*, and the other bit means *science*. Now, of course, one might ask, "Why? Didn't feminism address this adequately?" What we are, in fact, seeing is that everybody's experience brings something distinct to the table. In the body of the theory that I tried to convey, we are seeing that while we are talking about the loss of freedom of a gender, it is much more than that. Therefore, it is not about a very narrow gender equality. This movement doesn't particularly like that term, in any case. It doesn't like the term *gender equality*, because men are not free, so why would women want to be their equals. This is why the analysis is based on moral and political society. To seize surplus product required the development of multiple forms of enslavement of one by another, so seeing the women's enslavement only in terms of her physique simply doesn't cut it. It was an attack on the mindset and the order of things created by women that led to women's enslavement. Therefore, it is much more profound, and this is why it has been much more difficult to clearly illuminate what has been going on. This is why it is important that all of these struggles are unified.

Of course, there are duties that come with jineolojî and the sociology of freedom. It is not just research into history. What to do intellectually and economically, how to address rebuilding of political and social institutions, and how to free science and knowledge from the hands of monopolies must also be determined. Education of men by women is also another important aspect that the women's movement has been addressing for some time, both in the case of male revolutionaries within the Kurdish freedom movement and in society at large: revolutionaries and civilians at the same time. To make sure that that transformation occurs they discuss and question everything from what death is and how it is constructed and reconstructed to what a woman is and how we actually define a woman, how we define a man—and that is only the beginning. All of these discussions are very lively and are occurring right now. In fact, it is a fusion of both unearthing past memories and knowledge and of discussing what our new beings are like and how that can be transformed over time using different and constantly evolving institutional tools. This is why the Kurdish women's freedom movement increasingly involves the concept of *xwebûn*, which means *to be yourself*, drawing upon *xwe-parastin*, which means *self-defense*, and other forms of *xwe* (*self*). All these terms were introduced by Abdullah Öcalan, jineolojî first being mentioned in volume 3, *The Sociology of Freedom*, and xwebûn around the same time.[1] The women's freedom movement has constantly been developing, evolving, and implementing its contents.

This is very important. This is why the women's freedom movement has called for "eternal divorce." And this is perhaps why the PKK revolutionaries do not engage in sexual relationships. What we are seeing is that the relationship between men and women is deemed to be a private domain, but it is, in fact, the first and foremost locus of the colonization process. To be able to unravel that and be able to have these discussions more objectively without playing on emotion and creating space for women to just belong first to themselves, they begin their practice by first building their own space and organization. Xwebûn allows for a much stronger union and for them to develop a greater knowledge of themselves.

Feminism is the most important source for jineolojî, as it has immense experience in and value for the struggle for social liberation. Of course, jineolojî directed its initial efforts to investigating, analyzing, and evaluating women's enemy, patriarchal class civilization, and capitalist modernity. The criticisms of feminism and of the existing women's movements arose from a perspective that regards the problems pinpointed as its own and actively tries to find solutions. Progress is found in the ability to engage in self-criticism and reflection. Therefore, when feminism is criticized, it is with the aim of initiating a process of renewing a progressive dynamic. Indeed, there is an urgent need to start these discussions and to deepen them where they have already begun. The critique made does not ignore the hardships of or devalue the intellectual awareness created by the feminism that developed from the major struggles of women and their labor and pain around the world. However, one critique addresses feminism's fragmented epistemologies. While each feminist epistemology addresses a different domain, the question of why we have so many feminist epistemologies remains. Jineolojî points out that we should be critical and observe the methods of fragmentation as women organize themselves. However, this is not to be done in the competitive sense of the patriarchal culture but to facilitate a shared understanding that encompasses all of us and our different experiences and allows us to work together.

Another issue is the effect of orientalism on feminist theory, despite the fact that feminist theory has developed a significant critique of capitalist modernity. The effects of orientalism can be seen not only in the case of feminist theory but everywhere, including in the Middle East itself. Therefore, jineolojî finds it of utmost importance to expose the orientalist influences and struggles against them. When feminist academics do research, it is necessary that they question how preliminary assumptions of the social sciences generate orientalism.

Organizing is another issue. Despite the immense knowledge feminism has created, it has not played a sufficient role in or taken adequate responsibility for addressing the urgency and scope of society's need for social change and transformation. This is why feminist currents cannot be seen as an "alternative mainstream" by either society or statist power systems. These currents are more generally seen as "hope movements," i.e., movements that create hope. Although these currents present a theoretical critique of modernity, their inability to develop an alternative model of life that transcends the limits of modernity is something that we should keep in mind.

Another area of critique concerns ignoring sexuality as a domain of power. In nature, the existence and continuity of all living beings is ensured through nutrition, protection, and reproduction. Reproduction, in the case of human society, has been identified with sexuality and the unvalued labor of women. At the same time, in capitalist modernity sexuality has gone beyond reproduction for the continuity of existence and has been transformed into a domain of power. Women's sexuality has been controlled to implement power and guarantee its continuity. Instead of defining sexuality and its social meaning disconnected from its position of power, it has been conserved as an area that one is "free to choose." Since the 1970s, radical feminism and lesbian feminism have produced knowledge that deciphered the link between sexuality and power. These were efforts to identify with women's bodies and sexualities. Pornography was criticized as a capitalist product that trafficked in women. However, after the 1990s, these analyses, which departed from these points over time, fell into the traps laid by capitalism. "Sexual freedom" is treated as an individual matter, making it impossible to develop a culture of sexuality free from dominance and slavery. Therefore, jineolojî is trying to create a deeper understanding of sexuality, sexual identities, and relationships.

We talked about the need for the transformation of men earlier, to point out that feminist politics has primarily advocated the formation of women-only spaces, without paying much attention to also developing policies and common platforms for gender struggle that target the transformation of men. Unfortunately, feminist theory has not yet managed to get beyond being a movement that mostly resists and refuses. Feminist theory has not sufficiently focused on perspectives for the transformation of men.

How history is approached raises another issue, both in terms of recent and distant past: Should we or can we present women's experiences through the prisms of postcolonial feminism, Kurdish feminism, or Islamic feminism? To what degree do these currents represent the struggles of women in different regions of the world?

The main argument that has been put forward for the formation of jineolojî and, hence, for the emancipation of women and society as a whole is the need to link the philosophy of freedom movements with the study of social sciences. If we want society to be free, we must also free the social sciences from the control of the forces in power and reorganize them in the interest of the people.

Jineolojî, after initially being proposed by Abdullah Öcalan, was quickly embraced by the women's freedom movement, and, since 2011, discussions, implementation, and evolution of its content have carried on against the backdrop of the experience of the Kurdish women's freedom movement. It is defined as the science of women, the science of life, the science of how to live together. It is, in fact, the social science that Kurdish women's revolution rests upon. The sexist character of not only the social sciences but of all sciences necessitates woman's science. This is not only because they remain insufficient unless and until women's reality is clarified, but also because the way in which they describe and explain society will continue to be wrong. We are seeing that each and every scientific examination that takes into account women's reality reveals things that we have not acknowledged before— because women's reality and communality are so thoroughly intertwined.

Another responsibility of social sciences is to define life. This embraces content that goes beyond simply addressing the essence of being animate on the basis of the laws of physics and biology. We know that religions, mythologies, and philosophy all searched for an answer to this larger question. It is a wonder that this discussion has not been taken up by science. This has left a huge vacuum and crippled our understanding of life and our ability to make sense of it. Thus, Öcalan consistently emphasizes that there is a need to reunite philosophy and science. I guess, in this sense, as with the link that ancient languages and cultures make between women and life, jineolojî searches for the same meaning in this link, in this connection.

To end the destruction created by modernity's attacks on society's and women's history, spirit, and evolution, on our worlds of emotion and thought, on our female and human values and all the truths that make us who we are, the Kurdish women's freedom movement proposes jineolojî to create different forms of knowledge and wisdom. There is no life without meaning! But women's perspectives must develop without interrupting the connections between meaning, life, society, and women. Thus, they define jineolojî as the science of democratic modernity. We will have more to say about that later. As such, jineolojî also has the mission to play a role in building democratic modernity. The process of revolutionary reconstruction of science, its reconnection with society, and its dedication to animate, protect, and defend society must be led by society itself.

In the story of the formation of women's identity, there is a connection between quantum and chaos moments and jineolojî. The women's freedom movement says that this is the answer to the question: "What is jineolojî?" It's purpose is to analyze the freedom hidden in moments of creation, liberation, and life, and to contribute to building democratic modernity. It is the ability to create scientific, philosophical, and activist vehicles to express women's potential, in alliance with the other forces of democratic modernity. For this re-creation, they have declared, "In the Middle East, where many of the first inventions of social life emerged with women's justice, the women's spindle turns once again today to braid jineolojî!"

Jineolojî is already considered to be the energy, soul, and foundation of the sociology of freedom and has already become one of its most stable pillars, bringing about the very much needed revolution and providing the ethical point of departure for social sciences.

In terms of methodology, one of the important critiques advanced by jineolojî targets rationalism, positivism, and the subject-object distinction. What it criticizes about rationalism is that analytic intelligence and rational thought are not decisive or sufficient to understand truth. The struggles of women and of all colonized peoples have unearthed other aspects of the truth. Nonetheless, according to analytic intelligence and rational thought, sources other than the Western rationality are irrational and nonintellectual.

Over time, with philosophy playing a particular role, rationality came to be defined and described as male, and women were totally excluded. Irrationality was attributed to women, colonized peoples, the oppressed, and the poor, making them all interchangeable. The fundamental critique of rationalism is that analytic intelligence has been made devoid of moral values, empathy, and social responsibility, which allows for genocides, femicides, and the destruction of nature. We all have an acceptable tolerance level for what is going on. There is, thus, a need to develop a synthesis of analytic and emotional intelligence.

Of course, jineolojî also critiques positivism for the idea that problems can be resolved mathematically, rationally, or empirically, noting that any problem that cannot be resolved in this way is simply declared a "fake problem." This turned society into something like a laboratory. Measured. Supervised. Controlled. And we are seeing that nothing really works that way. In fact, the distinction between subject and object drew sharp borders that divided thought, perception, and social life, which easily lent itself to the creation of hierarchies. Rather than a distinction between subject and object, the two needs must be unified in each of us. The two must be fused. Too much emphasis on being a subject automatically turns the other into an object. As Öcalan points out in *The Sociology of Freedom*: "In the central civilization systems, the subject always stems from capital and power. It represents consciousness, discourse, and free will. At times, it is an individual, and, at other times, it is the institution, but it always exists. The objects are the barbarians, the peoples, and the women excluded from power. They are only thought of—as is the case with nature—when they serve the subject as a resource. Given the nature of things, no other meaning is imaginable for them. In Sumerian mythology, the creation story of the human being as a servant made from the excrement of the gods and of the woman made from the man's rib reflect the dimensions of objectification in the depths of history. The transfer of this subject-object approach to European thought required significant transformations." Jineolojî is removing the former statuses affixed to women like that of "sacred mother," someone's "honor," and the "indispensable partner" and trying to explore the reality of women as the subject-object sum. The most important dimension of this research is to expose the viciousness disguised under *love*.

Knowledge, on the other hand, was turned into a tool of power above the social structure, and its distribution was controlled to maintain this cycle. Every imaginable theoretical infrastructure was developed to distance society from the possibility of producing and constructing knowledge for itself. This infrastructure was oriented toward an ideological formation to regulate society. This scientific-technical rationale of domination of nature and society turned science into ideology, with positivism as its religion. Acquisition of this knowledge evolved into domination of nature, society, and women.

Several dichotomies are necessary to perpetuate control, including, body/soul, black/white, alive/dead, god/subject. All of them are necessary to control society and people. Therefore, we see the gradual development of patriarchal hegemony, followed by class hegemony, accompanied by racism, colonialism, etc., all of which this form of thought legitimizes. When we look at the time of the god-kings, and then the period of the non-human gods, we can see that the first distinction is already there. Division of the supernatural in terms of a "male god" and his subjects, which then expands into classes and other forms, gaining legitimacy in the process. In terms of nature, the former understanding of a living nature was replaced by nature as a dead object and the human as the divine subject. When this is the case, scientists feel they have the freedom to conduct unlimited experiments and do as they wish with nature. There are no moral issues that arise due to this mindset, and this objectifying approach to nature, women, and all the "others" sets the conditions for the unlimited "use" and disposal of anything/anyone. In fact, scientism with its object-subject distinction and "objectivity" has turned into an anti-society and misogynist force. Jineolojî, therefore, is a science of women and life that aims to set this right, because, in the end, we, as human beings, are social beings.

In reality, there is, of course, a distinction between the way women are enslaved and the exploitation of classes and peoples. The difference is that the oppression of women is legitimized through games and the manipulation of women's emotions. It is disguised as love or care or whatever. Therefore, it is much harder to deal with. There has been an attempt to turn the constructed weaknesses of women into a reality, thereby institutionalizing it. A systematic enslavement accompanied by all of the necessary institutions works twenty-four hours a day to ensure this institutionalization. Family is where this process begins and is part of the necessary institution-alization. Of course, all of this is presented in greater depth both in Öcalan's books and in the pamphlets and other texts on jineolojî that was prepared by the jineolojî committee and women's movement at large.[2]

Naturally, another issue is jineolojî's scope of action. The approach taken circulates around the idea that if jineolojî finds solutions to the problems of social life, then it is on the correct path. Jineolojî can maintain its claim of being a science as long as it acts to end the mentality and the sovereignty of the patriarchal institutions that have infiltrated every moment and every field of our life. That is to say, it must develop science as common wisdom, conscience, and action of society without falling into scientism.

There are a number of areas of concern, ethics and aesthetics among them. Öcalan says, "Ethics is the morality and consciousness of freedom. Aesthetics must emanate in line with this consciousness." Economy is another critical area. It is the economy that forces society, and women, to surrender. Demography is another significant area. Jineolojî, in contrast to the Malthusian theory, which was established as a means of patriarchal and capitalist state governance and social control, aims to develop and organize an alternative demographic understanding based on women's self-determination. Alongside ecology, history, and health care, there is also the important sphere of education. Jineolojî seeks to make the concept of *perwerde*—a Kurdish word for education related to an expression that means *to turn with love*—vital and to make sure that this process does not totally break away from society and women.

When it comes to politics Öcalan says, "If the function of morality is to accomplish the best of the tasks regarding life, the function of the politics is to determine what the best tasks are." Understanding politics as it is thought of by state civilization reproduces the habit of using politics as a means of deception and oppression, ensuring that society will always be kept out of politics, while at the same time being an object of politics. To avoid this, society and individuals need to equip themselves and strengthen their own minds. The task of jineolojî comes to light at this stage: preparing society and individuals for the realm of politics in terms of changing their own mindsets too. Jineolojî is ultimately a science that is being developed to achieve a free society and free individuals.

At the same time, jineolojî questions the meaning of life and explores how to live. First of all, we need to have a vision of life, of living, and of relationships that is different to that of capitalism. This, says Öcalan, is where "capitalism has been successful." He says, "In the past, if somebody was poor, they would revolt. But today, everybody hopes to win the lottery." Therefore, what's changed is that we now want to be in the place of the oppressor. Speaking generally, nobody wants to get rid of the oppressors. Even in the movies you don't see who does the housework. Revolutionaries, people who are struggling, and people who are committed to democracy need to have a vision of life and living that differs from that of capitalism.

In all of this self-defense is extremely important. The mainstream presentation in the US of women's self-defense units has generally focused on the fact that women are armed, but self-defense is not limited to physical defense. They are, of course, living in a very dangerous part of the world where everybody who intervenes does so with guns. There is a long history of the development of armed struggle by Kurdish women joining the ranks of the PKK and how and why they created women-only armies within the PKK. Partly, it's to do with how men make a big thing out of it. It is similar to how they even do so when they come home from work: that whole "I'm the breadwinner" thing. This reverberates at every level of activity and life. It also has to do with fact that they had to protect themselves. Under difficult circumstances and under attack it is particularly important that you don't sit around and wait for someone to protect you—it just may not happen for one or another reason. Thus, while women's self-defense units were a tool of equality within the ranks, they were also an important aspect for women to protect themselves against attacks. Self-defense, however, does not just addresses the physical side of things but everything I've been talking about, like uncovering women's history, education, health, arts, aesthetics.

Of course, we also have to redefine aesthetics and beauty for ourselves. We also see from the past that the first thing that changes is the culture around women. Looking at feudalism or capitalism, we see that beauty and what it means to be a woman is defined by men. As part of discussions of jineolojî, the definition of beauty, as well are who is a woman, are among the topics discussed. These discussions, as well as the immediate conditions of life and the results of action taken by women in the region, are giving rise to numerous methods for breaking down the mechanisms of power and hierarchy. Autonomous women's groups, movements, and institutions have grown first within the PKK and, in parallel, increasingly in society as well, to the degree that they have equal influence and power. Not only equal, in fact; when it comes to deciding on things in their autonomous movement and institutions they make their own decisions. They decide together what women should do, how they should do it, and who should go where when assigning women revolutionaries their duties and posts.

Women do not exist only as individuals. Excessive individualization of members of the oppressed is intentional. The system tries to turn all of us into nothing more than individuals and imposes this most harshly on women, the colonized and, of course, workers. Only men are really organized—and only if they have embraced their mold, because, as we note, the state is a male institution—the highest form of the male institution.

In the past, I remember they used to say of Kurds, "If two Kurds meet, they will fight," which indeed made it difficult for the Kurds to come together to decide on things. The idea was that if they didn't meet—and they shouldn't—they wouldn't talk to each other in any meaningful way, so they wouldn't be able organize. The state and its institutions did everything they could to make sure Kurds could not find ways of making decisions together. This can be extended to women. They used to say, "If two women meet, they will gossip." In this case, the idea was that we should not meet, we should not share, and we should not organize and act together. Of course, the purpose of meeting should not be to complain but to rid ourselves of the personality that has been forced upon women, the oppressed, and the colonized. Women in the Kurdish freedom movement and in the societal organizations are, in fact, highly organized. That is the source of their power. Their decisiveness, effectiveness, and influence are based on that organizational power.

Now for a brief history of jineolojî up to this point. In 2011, the women within the women's freedom movement formed a research unit and had intense discussions that lasted until 2013. First, the women discussed among themselves, followed by mixed discussions. Proposals were made and questions asked and discussed. A pamphlet was prepared. In the meantime, there were other discussions taking place as well. In Cologne, in 2014, there was a conference to introduce jineolojî, and other discussions were held throughout both North and Southern Kurdistan.

In 2015, the very first conference discussing and establishing how the freedom movement envisaged jineolojî. There, the basis was laid for jineolojî. Then a book introducing jineolojî was collectively prepared.[3] The next step was to make sure that jineolojî was integrated into all the freedom movement's educational endeavors. In Northern Kurdistan, a jineolojî academy, a journal, and research groups were established, and the space for its development and implementation was available in Rojava. A jineolojî committee was set up to undertake a social research project examining the Rojava revolution and, to that end, societal research was conducted in Shengal, Cizîrê, Kobanî, and Afrin. A jineolojî faculty at Rojava University and a jineolojî academy were set up in Rojava. Women's research centers were established in Derik, Kobanî, and Afrin. A women and children-only village called Jinwar, made by women for women, has been established. In Jinwar, as well as in all of the academies in Rojava—women, mixed, youth, and all others, and there are many academies—everyone is given an education on jineolojî. In Manbij, for example, an academy has been opened with and for Arab women specifically.

The jineolojî committee and academy examine all school-books and engages in dialogue to correct any religionist, posi-tivist scientist, sexist, or nationalist mindsets and narratives. There is also special education for those who are in positions of responsibility (teachers, self-defense units, *asayiş*,[4] justice, the economy, health care, etc.). All works of reconstruction, all meetings, every discussion, any court case where social prob-lems are resolved are followed and analyzed so that jineolojî can play a role in correcting errors in approach or mindset.

As you can see jineolojî is actually neither purely theoreti-cal nor merely practical. Instead, it works to overcome this dis-tortion of science. It reveals women's roles and contributions as founders, maintainers, and developers of society, in order to develop the meaning of social life. Realizing this requires a scientific approach—a science that has reunited with philoso-phy—that goes "beyond propaganda and demagogy."

These new institutions, established in Rojava, for example, are reviewed almost daily, so that they can be transformed as needed and as problems or developments occur. When we talk about institutionalization, we don't mean it in a negative sense but in the form of an organization that can also ignite and inspire development and carry it forward. This becomes the soul of the paradigm. The way in which women are enslaved is replicated in every other form of enslavement. Without cor-recting this, there can be no freedom—not even for men and certainly not for society. I'm going to leave it at that and hope-fully the questions will allow to delve more deeply into these issues. Thank you.

Q: *It's wonderful to hear about jineolojî. I have Mary Daly's Gyn-ecology in my head at the same time.[5] I was wondering if you could say a little bit about the Neolithic period. Mary Daly's theory of ecology understands it as at the center of women's*

understanding of human nature and connection. I'm think-
ing about grain empires being a significant change from the
Paleolithic to the Neolithic, and that women needed to be put
down because of this new way of living and ensuring people's
sustenance—that change. I know that there is an ecological sen-
sibility in the Rojava approach. Could you elaborate a little more
on that? I literally wonder: What are people eating in Rojava?

Havin: I was there four months ago. Wheat is the main crop,
of course. The Syrian regime was pretty brutal in the way it
divided food production into regions. This is another way of
actually stripping society of its ability to determine its relationship with nature. For example, in the canton of Jazira,
wheat is the main food crop grown. You see huge wheat depots.
Amazing. And they are like huge banks. I was told that they are
still eating the wheat from I don't know how many years ago. In
a way, that was beneficial for them during the war, but, apart
from that, they were not really allowed to do much else. There
is also cotton, especially in the Al-Hasakah region. Cotton and
wheat were basically the two crops grown there. And you have
olives in Afrin. So it was pretty much separated. This had a
huge impact on the soil, the repetitive growth of two crops—
I'm not an agriculturalist, but I can imagine the kind of damage
this does.

There was no shortage of food. A number of delegations
have been there and this is one of the things that people are
most surprised about. But I think what happened is that, in
general, the movement there was very quick to make sure
that, despite war conditions, the revolution is not strangled by
economic shortages or food shortages. Therefore, there is an
active effort to ensure wheat production as well as the production of other crops to make sure that they are not dependent on
imports from elsewhere. However, this year was a particularly
bad year, because there wasn't much rain, unfortunately, and
so there will be a shortage this year, from what I understand.
But they are trying to develop a lot of different agricultural

products and to resume that in the different regions. There is a major effort to form different cooperatives and to make sure that the different cantons share the various products they produce, like the soap and the Afrin olive oil. Afrin was invaded and is now occupied by Turkey. Let me come back to your point about jineolojî: our problem was that the only science of women, gynecology, addresses women's health problems, and that itself was a very late development, in any case. So, instead of being about that, it is basically about where we are coming from and where we want to go.

I am not really familiar with Mary Daly's work, but women's enslavement is not the result of a biological weakness or anything of the sort. It's not about that. It's about the order and morality she brings to bear on society's relationship with nature and on our relationships with each other to prevent hegemony or control over the surplus product. Let me give you an example. It may make things clearer. One day, I realized that we were indigenous people as well! That we all are actually! Although some of us had that memory repressed much earlier as a result of the rise of the society of the state, which separated us from our former way of living. One day, I asked my mother, "Mom, what did you do when there was no rain?" I thought, as we are indigenous, maybe we went out to the nature and did something together. She said, "What happened was everybody who had surplus food in their homes after they would put away what they needed for a year, would take that surplus food and go to the poorest home in their village. As a community, they would cook, eat together, and leave whatever is left cooked and uncooked in that house and go home. I was amazed. It was so natural for her, she did not see anything unusual about it. I was amazed to see how at the time people knew that the reason there was no rain was related to the injustice and inequality in their society—and, in this, animism, the way they relate to nature, must have played a role. They believed that it would rain if they remedied that. If they actually shared what they had, they would remedy the situation. So, yes, we definitely agree with that, the way to make it work is by reestablishing the necessary mechanisms, and by making moral and political society, which are constantly being damaged by state structures, functional again. More on that tomorrow, though.

Q: *You talked a little bit about how a number of autonomous women's groups have sprung up, beginning in the PKK, then spreading to other areas. One of the most interesting things for me when studying Rojava was to read about the women's tribunals and the councils and committees that they have created for themselves at every level of governance. I was wondering if you could talk about that a little bit and about the societal impact of incorporating women into every aspect of sociopolitical life in Rojava.*

Havin: Let me go back a little bit further and start with the freedom movement and with the PKK. Revolutionary women began to have their own autonomous meetings within the PKK. I think it was back in 1995 that they began to have separate organizational meetings, where women came together wherever they were to discuss the problems that they were having, as well as the problems associated with the social development in general, and ways of remedying them. I remember hearing from women at the time that the men were very curious and could not understand the reason for separate meetings. They were wondering what the women were doing in these meetings. But, of course, these meetings allowed women to develop policies that they then turned into theory, as well as organizing to combat and remedy the situations that they found themselves in. One golden rule at the time—and it still continues to be a rule—is that those meeting are not just about criticizing men. They are also about women evaluating themselves, because if men are solely blamed, this also creates a bottleneck, and women won't be able to develop themselves. This is what the PKK also did in the case of the Kurdish people. They didn't just critique the Turkish state. Yes, at first, they critiqued the Turkish state ideology, but they also turned around and said to the Kurdish society, "Look at yourselves. There are things to be changed there as well." It is basically the same sort of a thing, with one difference. Women do not criticize one another in front of the men, because of men's divide and rule strategies. They do this in their own meetings.

This slowly developed and reverberated within society as well. The state saw that women joining the PKK and becoming guerrillas in the mountains was actually influencing society. They tried to stop it. They used a lot of the tactics they usually use. The Turkish state began to say, "The women are being abused. They are taken to the mountains and exploited sexually, and so on." The state tried to prove that by giving virginity tests to the women guerrillas who had lost their lives in combat. They tried to prove this was the case to stop the women going to the mountains. But these tactics failed to provide the desired results, and none of this really worked, because women organizing in this manner very quickly proved to also be an intervention into men's classic way of doing of things. Armed struggle, for example: it was always seen as a man's job or a man's thing, one that very quickly regresses and repeats the military conceptions of patriarchal civilization. This monopoly was broken by women's organizational development and presence in the armed struggle, and then things really began to change. Being organized allowed women to destabilize and change this backward equilibrium.

The women's organization started as a branch within the PKK, as was the case in other national liberation movements. But then as these questions were faced and taken seriously, rather than being ignored, the women's organization became truly autonomous. It was recognized that the male commanders would want to use their power to have influence over the women. It all unfolded under organizational mechanisms and in a comradely spirit. None of this meant that women and men were archenemies or opposed one another, but it was a wake-up call for the men as well. In general, the struggle was a very constructive struggle, although also very difficult and with its problems, and it's still going on today.

All of this has reverberated within society. There was a time when revolutionary women were valued in Kurdish society, but not women in general—not civilian women. There was also a phase early on when some women within the women's movement wanted to be like men, because they thought that was a way to be free. The women's movement went through different phases. As a result, now, in Rojava, there are also many different layers of organization that women participate in. One layer would be the young women who are autonomously organized in the youth organization. Women also come together in a general way, with their own spaces and organizational processes and procedures. That is also an experience they share. There are also many different layers to the women's tribunals as well: the justice system, in that sense. There are the women's houses that are the first instance of intervention into situations of violence, of abuse, whether physical or psychological, or any conflict of any kind. Then they have the power. . . Well, I don't want to say the power but influence, let's say, because it is very much accepted within society, to establish either educational or other ways of resolving the conflicts that occur in a given relationship.

It may seem like a paradox that this movement is very critical of the family but is not dissolving it. It may seem paradoxical, but they are looking at transforming the family, because they recognize that both in the capitalist societies and elsewhere, the family unit can also offer protection. It can be a constructive organizational unit as well. Traditionally, the Kurdish family was indeed very negative. This changed over the years, with the struggle. The Turkish state has steered the Kurdish family in such a way that it became an agent for the self-assimilation of the youth back into society. This is why, even today, the state calls on the family and mothers to take charge of the children to prevent them from engaging in revolutionary activity. If they love their children, then they should take charge of them. Although it may look paradoxical, the idea is that individuals are not left unprotected. Instead of completely dissolving the family, they are trying to transform it, by transforming both men and women and the education they receive, but, most of all, through the organization of women so that the power she has lost can be reinstated, strengthening her position within the family, so that there is more room in the family for transformation. Whenever there is a case involving a woman that involves a death, where somebody has been killed or murdered, etc., the judges involved are women, and they have the final say on these issues.

Q: *You talked about the use of dichotomies as a measure of patriarchal control over both people and society. I was wondering how the binary opposition between "man" and "woman" figures in this critique.*

Havin: Yes, I said that this is also being questioned. The reality the Kurdish people are in might be a lot different from the reality in the US. We have a conference in Hamburg every two years: Network for an Alternative Quest. David Harvey came, and we wanted him to speak on nation-states. He didn't, he spoke on banks, and we thought, "Hmm, okay, well that doesn't really mean much for us," because we have no banks in Kurdistan. So the realities or the emphasis or what is at the forefront can change, depending on the developmental stage you're at. In fact, this question comes up in many different ways. When I was in Stockholm, Sweden, somebody asked me, "What is the situation of LGBT people in Rojava?" "Well," I said, "Whatever the situation is in Stockholm, it's almost the same over there. There are those who accept it, and there are those who don't." But even *that* is being questioned, because capitalism handles many things by co-opting and appropriating them.

Now what we are seeing is the only way to be seen as a demo-cratic or a "progressive" is to accept this without any questions. That makes you a progressive. That's why we are seeing, for example, some of the most racist parties having either gay or lesbian ministers as a showy façade, as if that makes them progressive and democratic. The Kurdish freedom movement doesn't take anything on face value. This is why, in the case of jineolojî, and when discussing aesthetics and the like, I noted that all these systems, including feudalism, created and recre-ated what a woman and a man is. During feudalism in particu-lar, children—many of them—were necessary. It was all about agriculture and male physical power and working the land and whatever else. So there was greater emphasis on this, and it was brought to the forefront.

There is a need to acknowledge that at present we as people and our lives are created and structured in the way that will serve the functioning of the system we live in. What the Kurdish women's freedom movement and jineolojî are doing is questioning that anew and redefining what a woman is. Does it have to be biological? I don't know. There is a huge discussion and evaluation of the results of *doing*. Does it have to be that anyone who has breasts and this and that is a woman? What is the definition of *woman*? What is the definition of *man*? Do these definitions have to be so dogmatic? All of this is up for discussion at the moment. It's an area of exploration. I read a book about Iran that said that a couple. . . maybe a hundred years ago or so, a woman was considered beautiful if she had a little bit of moustache. This was seen as beauty at the time. Even sex itself is being questioned! Was sex itself really so sex-ualized? Was it everywhere, twenty-four hours a day like it is now? All of this is being discussed. And all these false feelings that are constructed, for example, the clock on motherhood: that you have to have a child. As I said, the approach of states change constantly according to their policies. Sometimes all of a sudden, the policy becomes that women have to have at least three kids, and families and mothers will receive money if they do—while at various times in different parts of the world there should be fewer children. We have to look at the construction of the different sexes, at the construction of sexes through these policies to control our surplus product or to make sure that there are enough people who can work in the factories.

They are trying to disentangle all of this, and it is going to take a while, I suppose. I mean, it took five thousand years to get here. I don't think we should have fancy ideas that all of a sudden things are going to begin to change very quickly. But that's why they are looking at the past and trying to combine it with what we have learned and know today, so that we can move on to tomorrow. It's a combination of all of that. I actually found it very interesting how it resonates, how the way PKK cadres live resonates with the old Kurdish tradition, especially the tradition that is still alive in the Kurdish Yazidi community. There are women in that community who by choice don't get married or, if they are married, some announce that they have reached such a spiritual level that they end their marriage and their husbands too become their believers. Society accepts them as cultural bearers of their community. The community is very responsive to their interventions. Now we are looking at the PKK cadres, and one of the particular ways they are unique is that they have made the rupture with the way that everybody else is living. They don't work for money. They don't have sexual relationships. The result is that there is no conflict of interest. This automatically gives them a certain authority, a moral authority, because people see that they are devoting their lives for no personal profit. It is almost like those cultural bearers. I wonder if there is any connection to or knowledge of this from the beginning. It's an interesting question. I only learned of this Kurdish Yazidi tradition very recently.

I know that at the moment the jineolojî unit in Rojava is doing major research into Kurdish society, into the societies in North Syria in general, addressing all of these different aspects.

What I'm trying to say is that there is much to be learned from the past, but, of course, we can't live in the past. When we talk about the Neolithic, it is in that sense; we are not saying, "Let's all go back to that stage" but, rather, we are asking, "What can we learn from it?"

Q: *I'm curious about the methodology. How did the early Kurdish freedom movement get men who are the product of five thousand years of patriarchy and five hundred years of capitalism to start giving up that control? Most groups in control never want to share it or give it up.*

Havin: They are not giving it up. Don't you worry. It's not that easy!

Q: *It just seems like such a monumental task to get people who are in control, whether through race, religion, sex, gender, whatever, to even begin to have that conversation.*

Havin: One important aspect is that the movement didn't come to this conclusion from day one. Therefore, everybody moved forward together. It was a collective learning, collective discussion, collective moving together, moving ahead together. I think this is invaluable—this method. I don't know if I talked about it yesterday, but the way education occurred inside the organization was extremely transparent. You would have, let's say, three hundred people, not all of them cadres, people from civil society—the sympathizers too—would also come to that school. It's an oral tradition. It would be talking. There would be an analysis. There would be a discussion. There would be critique. And this would all be taped, and then these tapes would go to Kurdish homes. The families—the young, the old, the men, the women—would all watch. The problems of the revolution would be discussed in that room of three hundred people, and the results of problems—the consequences of the incidents, events, and situations experienced—would be analyzed and discussed. Tools, institutions, organizations that could stop the perpetuation or continuation of these problems would also be discussed. It would become a collective thing. This process would be more or less repeated in other parts of the world within Kurdish society. Thus, the evaluation of that one incident and the way to resolve it as an example would reach everyone, the sympathizers and cadres alike, and it would be on everyone's agenda. Therefore, you would try to overcome problems together. With the women's movement, or women's freedom, it's the same thing, because there have been many, many great women who have carried forward and developed the Kurdish freedom movement, both in theory and in practice. The Kurdish people are witnesses to that. Kurdish men are witnesses to that. If you go back in time, there are very famous male revolutionaries, but there are also many women revolutionaries who have made a leap, both theoretically and in terms of practice, in the movement and in society.

I heard of a very good example. Let me share it. When the cadres would go to the school, Öcalan would be there, and it would be old and new cadres, revolutionaries, men, women, civilians, whatever. It would be a mixed group. And it would usually be half and half. Women would not do any of the cleaning or the cooking in that setting, and the men would very quickly get upset about that. They would say, "We thought life was fifty/fifty. Why are we doing all the cleaning and the cooking, and the women are not doing any?" And, of course, these were the movement's house rules. I've heard that the women very intelligently and quite happily tried to explain, but the men wouldn't budge. The women would say, "Okay, go and tell comrade Öcalan. He is responsible for the house. Go and tell him, if you won't listen to what we are saying." They would go to Öcalan. They would say, "Comrade, what's going on? Why aren't women participating in the chores of cooking and cleaning?" And Öcalan would, of course, point out that they come from a life where they had been part of a family. Had they shared the cooking and the cleaning with their mothers and sisters or their wives, as the case might be. The house rule is that whoever had done less of something in the past would now do the more of it. Women traditionally do the cooking and the cleaning, so in this situation they will not do any of it. They will do what they would have been doing less of—politics, reading, discussing, talking, and everything else. And the men usually do the organizing and the talking, so they will do the cleaning and the cooking and the rest of that, so as to feel it and understand it, not to take it for granted, to actually do it and learn by doing it. All these things don't disappear over-night. This hegemony thing; patriarchy is very tricky. And men have to be very alert about this, because it gets refined. It gets really refined. This is why the movement has taken lots of different precautions, which is also true in the case of women. The way it has been done is complementary. There needs to be precautions taken in terms of institutions, decision-making mechanisms, etc. to address and, finally, completely eradicate the problem.

It's not easy, and, at times, there have even been reactions against it. In fact, this is why I said at the beginning that women are especially appreciative of Öcalan. It is because of his radical comradeship, despite the fact that, at times, there have been reactionary male responses targeting Öcalan around this point. I think we currently have to be especially careful about this male chauvinism. As we discussed yesterday, at the moment, all the reactionary rulers around the world are calling upon the men to again take charge. So this is important.

Q: *My question is about listening and watching. It strikes me that this seems, in many ways, certainly in the Middle East, to be a pro-found new development. I'm also struck by how similar, in terms of practice, not in terms of ideas and the way things are framed, this is to the things that I've learned about the revolutions of the twentieth century, where women's questions were a huge com-ponent. We have a way of looking back at the Marxist verbiage* *of these revolutions and saying maybe they were looking at class but not gender. Then you read about the Chinese Revolution and even the way that the Chinese Communist Party engaged the self-activity of women to overthrow the feudal patriarchal structures in the villages. It was in so many ways strikingly similar to the things that you see happening now, or at least what appears to be happening. It's hard to tell by watching things through* Vice news *and the like. I'm really curious about how you see that question of the history of women's struggles within revolutions, and what in practice makes what's happening now different, because obviously we can see that the ideas are different. But what are the differences in practice? Thank you.*

Havin: First of all, they do not see the oppression and exploitation of women as a gender issue alone. It is, of course. First and foremost, it's the women who experience the backlash and the violence, the oppression of all of this. But, as I said, this theory exposes the fact that women are the first class. The usual division is: class oppression is distinct; women's exploitation is distinct; the colonization of Indigenous peoples is distinct. This is not how they see it. They see the enslavement of women as the formation of the first colony, the first class. All of the others descended from this. So the downfall of women is actually the downfall of the order that didn't allow for class division. Because this is perhaps not properly conveyed, because this is not really understood, it can, at times, be thought that the issue of class is not addressed. On the contrary, it is addressed at its roots and in all its variety.

If we look back, even to the time of the Nimrods, of the god-kings, there were internal struggles within the Abrahamic religions, which, if you look at them on their own, are not progressive. However, if you look at them in terms of a struggle with the god-king system, they are reformist. What I'm trying to say is that there are struggles both within the system (for example, the working class) and the struggle of those who are excluded from the system (for example, the colonized and women). These struggles are of a whole cloth. One is internal colonization, and, at the end of the day, they are not so distinct from one another. As a result, of course, both the Kurdish freedom movement and the women's freedom movement have learned a lot from past struggles. One important lesson was that after the revolution women were sent back home by their male comrades. Why? They posed that question. Why is this the case?

In fact, it had already happened without the Kurdish freedom movement becoming a state. Some of the commanders wanted to send the women back to society because staying in mountains was difficult. This is why the Kurdish freedom movement doesn't believe in any "after the revolution." Revolution is continuous. It is instantaneous. One aspect of the PKK's methodology is that you do while you think, and you think while you do, so that you may be able to catch the moment of transformation and transform yourself and the society with you. It doesn't happen overnight. They didn't turn into this movement overnight either. Therefore, questioning things anew, restructuring, changing the tools, altering the institutions and organizations, mechanisms that will carry this forward is what is important.

I think this is what sets the Kurdish freedom movement apart, actually: the fact that their approach rests on feminism. Feminism has done an amazing job. We shouldn't forget that. It has made the women's question visible. But what is now being said is that one needs to go a step further and to define the kind of a society that is envisaged. It's not enough to define women as oppressed. This is why you've probably heard of *Jin Jiyan Azadi*. Because of this theory, more often than not, the Kurdish freedom movement has shown the connections that make women's revolution the liberation of life itself. It is about freeing life. Therefore, men also see that, in fact, they do not have any real privileges. Similarly, we say that the colonization and oppression of Kurds prevents Turks from becoming democratic. The enslavement of women also perpetuates the enslavement of men. It is all hand in glove. All efforts are made to expose this, to show this. That's why we say women's revolution liberates life. In Kurdish, the root of the word *life* is *Jin*. *Jin* means *woman*, while *jîn* means *alive* and *jiyan* means *life*. The root word is the same. And that's why we say Jin Jiyan Azadi. *Azadi* means *freedom*. And given that the Sumerian word for freedom is *Amargi*, which means *returning to mother*, the three words are so interconnected and make perfect sense: women, life, freedom. As women becomes free, it is inevitable that life itself will return to its magic and enchantment. Thus, the slogan *Jin Jiyan Azadi*.

Notes

1 Abdullah Öcalan, *The Sociology of Freedom: Manifesto of the Democratic Society*, vol. 3 (Oakland: PM Press, 2020).

2 See Jineoloji, accessed February 7, 2021, http://jineoloji.org/en.

3 Jineoloji Akademisi, *Jineolojiye Giriş* (Diyarbakır: Aram Yayınları, 2015). An abridged English translation was published as Jineolojî Committee Europe, *Jineolojî*, 2nd ed. (Neuss: Mezopotamien, 2018), accessed February 7, 2021, https://jineoloji.org/en/wp-content/uploads/2018/05/Jineoloj%C3%AE-English-v2-Final.pdf.

4 Local self-defence units that are responsible for neighborhood security and are bound by the decision-making mechanisms of the local assemblies.

5 Mary Daly, *Gyn-Ecology: The Metaethics of Radical Feminism* (Boston: Beacon Press, 1978).

LECTURE III

Democratic Confederalism and Democratic Nation—Defense of Society against Societycide

The previous two nights have been pretty important in allowing us to present the soul of the political and social system that the Kurdish freedom movement and Abdullah Öcalan are proposing. What we said, and this is important, is that they not only problematize capitalist modernity and patriarchy, but, as they are not just intellectuals or academics, they also have certain responsibilities. Abdullah Öcalan is not just an intellectual or a prisoner on an island, but, as the guide or leader of the Kurdish people, it was also his responsibility to propose something. If that something is not capitalist modernity, then what would it be?

Last night, we examined how slavery was actually constructed or built. We saw that a narrative is of the utmost importance, especially when it comes to colonizing or enslaving women or peoples. Whether psychologically or historically, a history that strips them of their power and strength and objectifies them must be established. We saw that this was extremely important. What the Kurdish freedom movement does, in that sense, is to create unity in the fragmented histories of women, peoples, and those who have been struggling for freedom for the last five thousand years or so, because the history that we have today is the history of the rulers. We have remarked, and maybe you have also noted this, that in the last ten to fifteen years, there have been an increasing number of books about what happened to the people, what happened to the women, during those five thousand years. Öcalan in his thirteen odd books from prison, which, as I explained, are submissions to the various courts, has unified and represented the history of all those who have been struggling as representatives of democratic civilization in opposition to the traditional patriarchal civilization. He is creating a corpus to address that. Thinking dialectically about democratic modernity, he believes that classic civilization cannot exist in the absence of democratic civilization. Therefore, democratic modernity is the dialectical counterpoint to capitalist modernity.

To be able to understand and deconstruct what has been happening, Öcalan is now looking at what the foundation of capitalist modernity is. When we look at that, we see that it is built on three pillars. The first, he calls the "society of the state," or "capitalist society," here meaning the mindset of competition and profit-seeking and not the economic system, the second, industrialism as we know it, and the third, the nation-state. He considers these to be extremely important dimensions, and he builds democratic modernity on three contrasting pillars. The first pillar he calls "moral and political society." We talked about that a little bit yesterday, noting that different forms of thought have looked at and analyzed history using different units. For example, capitalist modernity sees things from the perspective of the state, while Marxism uses class as a vantage point. In analyzing history, Öcalan takes moral and political society as the unit of analysis, placing women at the center of this society. When doing so, he looks at how the different state formations since the Sumerians have made a society of their own, rendering it dependent on the state. How was this done? How, in that process, did society become dysfunctional in terms of decision-making, in terms of very dynamically creating its own morals, morality, and rules, which changed over time, etc. And the political, as well: How was it lost?

If we examine the issue from the vantage point of our own time, what we see is that at the beginning, in the time of the Sumerians, for example, the embryo of the state was the ziggurats. The ziggurats physically embodied the structure of the state, with those who actually did the work located at the base of the ziggurat, working away. In the middle were the artisans, and at the top, the priests. Initially, there seemed to be not much violence used against the people. First, people were convinced of the legitimacy of this way of working, perhaps by what they read in the stars. The sun always rising in a particular place, the stars are where they are supposed to be, and this is why the world works so nicely. There was a lot of surplus product, so their way of working was very productive. Bit by bit, alongside this highly productive system, free society was being eaten away at. We note that as this process further developed in the period of the god-kings, there wasn't much violence within the society they ruled, but there were consistent attempts on the part of the tribes, the clans, and women to break away. In time, there were violent and nonviolent efforts to incorporate everyone into the god-kings' society: the society of the state.

With the rise of dynasties and empires, it remained the case that apart from the nobles and their servants or bureaucrats, those who remained outside were those who were unconquered. This is why empires had walls. We can still see these walls in many places around the world, especially in Europe and the Middle East. There was the society of the state and another society outside of the walls.

If we conduct an anthropology of the state and society through that lens, we see that by the time we arrived at the nation-state the process had become so far-reaching that almost all of society has been rendered dependent on the state. Whether through wage labor or the increasing loss of rural areas, we were increasingly losing our ability to remain independent of state structures. This is very important for the state, because if you are dependent on its structures, you will not try to get rid of it. Overall, this is a very important factor. We will talk a little bit more about that.

A key aspect of the concept of democratic confederalism and democratic autonomy is determining how to revitalize and reinvigorate moral and political society and make it functional again. It has been stripped of all of its functionalities. We are seeing this in many areas: in the area of health, for example, natural healing and medicine developed by women has been belittled in favor of the industrialization of health care. Clearly, the medicine and some aspects of the health services that have been developed by science are very important in some areas, but excessive industrialization and the elimination of preventative medicine has deprived society of so much. The fact is that health care has been restricted to industrialized medicine and society's knowledge and ability to address and remedy itself has almost been wiped out. The know-how no longer exists, at least to a great extent. I know this from our community and our society. My grandmother knew how to brace a broken leg, but now that isn't possible. Not only do we not know how; to all intents and purposes, we are not allowed to do so. This is also another area and another example of how we are totally stripped of our functionality.

Rather than industrialism, Öcalan's second pillar is ecological industry. It is not an opposition to industry but to industrialism, which is not only destroying the environment but is also turning everyone into a consumer and objectifying everything. The third pillar is democratic confederalism instead of the nation-state. We will now go into more detail about this.

We see how society is being enveloped by this nation-state and being stripped of its functionality and bureaucratized, with services that disguise the nature of the state—which is a sort of mafia that extorts resources in the form of taxes, by looting, or in any other possible way, disguising this with the services it renders, when actually it is we who do the work to provide these services, in any case. Furthermore, it is important to recognize that the state tries to implant law instead of morality, and instead of politics the state essentially establishes bureaucratic administration. It is important to see societal problems arise around the city, class, and the state structures that take shape around the essence of monopoly. The monopolization of all of these things is also extremely important. The problem we have with industry is that industrialism, in fact, chases profit. Were we to orient industry and technology in a way that benefited moral and political society, that would make our lives much easier. However, because it pursues profit and capital accumulation, and only for certain elites at that, it increases oppression and colonization and only generates accumulation for a certain number of people.

In response, we define the societal system of democratic modernity as democratic confederalism. Democratic confederalism is not limited or restricted to any ethnic area or region. There can also be regional democratic confederalisms. In Turkey, democratic autonomy is not only proposed for the Kurdish areas but for all areas of Turkey. Democratic confederalism is not only proposed for Kurdish populations but also for Arab populations that are separated by borders—approximately twenty Arab countries—and for Turkic peoples. Of course, it is not solely based on identity of ethnicity. Democratic confederalism is proposed for the whole of the Middle East. The idea here is neither to overemphasize ethnic identities nor to ignore them. In fact, a World Confederation of Democratic Nations is proposed to replace the United Nations, which represents nation-states rather than people.

The nation-state is capitalism's most fundamental tool for conquering and colonizing society. Without the nation-state, which is more powerful than all past forms of the state, it wouldn't have been possible. What we have is the upper layer of the middle class tied to the process of monopolization. This nation-state unifies all of the different past monopolies, including the industrial, financial, and military monopolies. All of these different monopolies, including the ideological monopoly, are gathered together in one place. In previous forms of state, you didn't find this level of monopoly.

The state form during the time of empires, for example, the Ottoman Empire, in fact, most empires, wasn't responsible for the education of everyone in the empire. With the capitalist nation-state, which is presented to us as very progressive, every child must go to school. This was a perfect way of creating individuals who would abide by the way of life that was imposed, because they would automatically understand the mindset. There would be no way of escaping it. This is the uniqueness of the nation-state. Fernand Braudel says, "power is accumulated like money."[1] Öcalan adds, "Power is the most refined and historically accumulated form of capital."[2] We are seeing that power, in fact, becomes more important than capital, ensuring that the nation-state is wrapped in much more armor than any former state. You have ideological, juridical, political, economic, and religious armor. Maybe you've read Hegel. He addressed the philosophy of state. He calls the state "the march of God in the world"[3]—the nation-state as "the march of God in the world."

On the other hand, as the nation-state becomes the maximum form of power, society is stripped of all of its functionality, which is transferred to the modern state. As such, society is stripped of its political strength and its economic existence. I can see that in the US; it's so much more profound than anything else I have seen, because there is so much dependency created, dependency on wage labor in particular. As you strip society of its political and economic strengths, it is much easier to eliminate them, physically or in some other way.

The nation-state not only seizes, conquers, and colonizes the material culture, or the resources, it also assimilates the moral culture. This is one of the most dangerous things about the nation-state. It homogenizes everything, and with the pretext of creating a national culture it makes the cultural norm of the dominant ethnicity and religion the general norm. This is not something that occurred in the past. I'm not saying that the earlier empires were great. We know how bad they were, and that people rebelled and struggled against the former forms of the state, but the nation-state, in making a single nation and, in most places, defining that nation on the basis of a single ethnicity, turned our world into a graveyard of cultures. It created emotional flashpoints that allowed it to incite peoples, cultures, and genders against one another, by, for example, making the homeland, its borders, and a flag sacred. You can then incite people. We see this in Turkey. Whenever the Turkish state wants to stir up nationalism and emotions, it has somebody burn a Turkish flag at a protest—we have frequently seen this in the past. Then suddenly there is no room for anything else, and all talk of democracy is abolished. How homeland is understood is also problematic. It is usually understood as a land with state borders, which is, in fact, based on the domination of capital within those borders by the various upper layers of the middle class. This makes controlling people's emotions with the extreme symbolism of geographic borders very easy.

On the other hand, we are seeing—and we talked about this a little bit on the first day—that these nation-states are very much dependent on and servants to the power centers of world capitalism. There is no independence in that sense. Öcalan calls this societycide. He says, "The greatest danger today, after genocides, after femicides, is societycide." He describes the nation-state as an octopus with its arms wrapped around each and every function of society, thus strangling society. Whether it's health, morality, politics, culture, reproduction, food. Paradoxically, as this increases, it's not particularly good for capitalism either. Capitalism always requires noncapitalist societies to colonize, if it is to get more by putting in less. Societycide must be understood as very, very dangerous. I will return to the subject when I talk about democratic autonomy and democratic confederalism and how the Kurdish freedom movement thinks this societycide can be overcome—how the octopus arms can be cut off to stop the suffocation of society.

Nation-states tried to homogenize society and, thereby, turn it into a mass. But we are seeing that this is actually creating a lot of problems on the ground. We took a glimpse at the description of a nation-state and how harmful and destructive this is. The mindset they want to instill has reached such a point that they want everyone to believe that the end of the world is near, and there is nothing we can do about it. I suppose this is where Rojava was a big surprise for the whole world. After the collapse of real socialism, people began to lose hope that there could ever be another way of living. Transnational capital and all those who turn the wheels of capitalism tried to make us believe that the world would come to an end, that they were looking for signs of life in the universe, in outer space, so we should give up on doing anything on earth. How clever: a new version of heaven and hell. There is a very active effort being made to this end. Why is that? So that we don't resist. So that we don't struggle. So that we don't think of new ways of doing things. That we, instead, participate in the depletion of the environment, of ecology, of each other, of society, of social relations, because the end is going to come anyway. Of course, this is not the case. This is an effort to deepen egoism, to deepen individualism and selfishness, so that we are unable to attempt anything else, and when we do we are not particularly successful if we are unable to address this egosim, individualism, and selfishness.

The political alternative is called democratic confederalism, and it is not an alternative state but an alternative to the state. The usual argument is that the state is the best coordinating body. If there is no state, we won't be able to manage our lives. However, there is an alternative to the state. How does it work? It is open to different and multilayered political formations. It maintains an equilibrium among central, regional, and local formations. It is based on a moral and political society of the sort that I've been talking about. Revolutions, however, do not create moral and political society. Revolutions: all they can do is cut the arms off the octopus or hold them off. Inevitably, everybody criticizes the concept of a revolution led by a vanguard, right? Because once the revolution succeeds it's all supposed to be over and "happily ever after," but throughout history we have repeatedly seen that this is not the case. What is being said is that revolutions should pave the way for society to become functional again. They should introduce institutions, organizations, and tools that can reinvigorate society. Over time, society, at its own pace and with its own dynamics, will become functional once again—but, of course, society must be organized within this process.

Democratic politics is extremely important, as is democratic governance and supervision of the work that goes on in society. Mechanisms must be established within society to address this. All of the various social groups and cultural identities will have political formations that allow them to express themselves. This is happening in Rojava. It was also happening in Northern Kurdistan, in Turkey, but it was crushed in a very violent manner. Northern Kurdistan is trying to revive itself as we speak. Their resistance continues. However, as you probably know, the growing fascism is Turkey has been legitimized by the German state's policies and support, as well as those of the United States to an even greater degree. Although there are contradictions between the EU countries, especially Germany and the US, as well as contradictions with Russia and China, for example, what they all share is the desire to colonize, exploit, and oppress. No matter how paradoxical it appears, they complement one another.

What they are trying to do in Rojava is to create society's self-governance. Remember, we talked about the analysis of how the society is being suffocated, and we have talked about how this enslavement began. We called women's enslavement the creation of the first class, first colony, and first nation. We talked about the youth. We talked about different peoples. We also talked about the working class. We talked about how the working class, in the society within capitalist countries, has also been colonized. What Öcalan is saying is that the way to reinvigorate society is to organize all those who have been excluded. Women build an autonomous organization so that they are able to make decisions for themselves and to examine and analyze history, the present, and the future. The same is true of the youth. The youth are also autonomously organized, and for the same reason: to be able to eliminate the oppressive and exploitative approaches taken to the youth. It doesn't stop there; the same is true for the communities of faith, for example, the Kurdish Yazidi community. You probably noticed that both ISIS and the Turkish state targeted and continue to target the Yazidi Kurdish community in Sinjar (or Shengal), while the Kurdish freedom movement, both the PKK and the movement in Rojava, tried to stop the genocide, and their approach in the aftermath of the attacks was to encourage the Yazidis to develop their own dynamics, to develop their own way of life, self-defense and all. These dynamics will not, however, be immune to criticism or guidance if this society or any other develops a pattern of oppressing women, for example. The intervention is critique-based, but it won't stop at saying, "Oh, you can't oppress women." It will also guarantee that women within the Kurdish Yazidi community are themselves autonomously organized. The same goes for the youth. This amounts to deconstructing the different power centers by making sure that those who have traditionally been exploited are organized and resist oppression, power, hierarchy, etc. through this self-organization. There is no vanguard in the classic sense, but there is guidance and active organization to build free life for all. You don't go to Kurdish Yazidi society and say, "I've come to free you." You provide the tools so that they can free themselves.

Self-defense can also be seen in that light, as can education. In Rojava, there is an education movement. It is not under the control of the Partiya Yekîtiya Demokrat (Democratic Union Party: PYD) or the Tevgera Civaka Demokratîk (Movement for a Democratic Society; TEV-DEM); it is independent. It is a movement in its own right, but it also has a place within the democratic autonomy structures from the grassroots level to the top, as well as regionally and at the level of the northeastern Syrian federation.

Health is approached in the same way.

All of this is meant to undermine the monopolization of these different spheres that suffocate the functionality of society. If you're ever in Rojava, you'll be amazed. We were there a couple of months ago. There are nonstop meetings, and there are education centers, communes, councils, and many different kinds of cooperatives.

This is also true for the Assyrian Christians. Some people wonder about the Arab community or the Assyrian community. There are, of course, some problems. The Assyrian and Arab communities are a bit cautious because of what will happen if the project is not successful, among other concerns. The Assyrian community is somewhat divided. There are those who have set up their own self-defense units to defend the Assyrian community. It follows that it is very important that the Assyrian community, like the Yazidi Kurdish community, not be dependent solely on the general self-defense forces—that self-defense is grounded in their own community. That will allow them to decide how to position and ground it and will give them control over it. The women's movement and other movements within the Assyrian community are, of course, also very important and encouraged to flourish.

There are, however, also sections of Assyrian society that are dependent on the Assad regime, and that would like to pull things in that direction. This is also true with the Kurds and the Arabs. These things are all ideologically based. With the Kurds, for example, as you know, there is the Partiya Demokrat a Kurdistanê (Kurdistan Democratic Party; KDP). There are other ideological formations, especially in Southern Kurdistan, that are trying to infiltrate Rojava to undermine this project, because if it succeeds and gains traction, their status—not the status of Southern Kurdistan—is at risk. There is a lot going on in Rojava in quite a number of ways, and it resonates throughout society in Iraqi Kurdistan. The people there are demanding similar developments in their society, which is causing unrest. In addition, their collaboration with the Turkish state poses a wide range of threats not only for the Kurds in Rojava, but for all Kurds, including in the south, as well as the north.

The mindset of capitalist modernity and the nation-state is reflected in the homogenization of everything within our lives. Instead of addressing complexities, we are obliged to embrace simplicity in many areas. Especially when it is good for profits, even when it comes to fruit and vegetables, right? I must admit, I saw a couple of different types of potatoes here. Usually, you have one type of carrot, even though the family of carrots is pretty large. The reason is simple: it's not profitable to produce them all. Everything is reduced to profitability and manageability, including people and languages. One of the arguments against having education in multiple languages is that it's too expensive. Everything is increasingly pushed under that lens, and, as the process unfolds, we begin to find it logical that numerous varieties of this or that cannot exist, that it's not feasible.

What they are attempting to develop in Rojava is an ability to make decisions on the basis of the discussion of these multi-layered organizations. The safeguard is the kind of organization that won't revert to how things were before, that all those who were traditionally oppressed are so well organized that they can't have what they've built stripped away from them. When decision-making takes place in discussions in these communes and/or councils, the traditionally oppressed arrive well-organized and ready to defend their case and to make sure that there will be no decisions to their detriment.

In democratic confederalism, one of the other principles is that there should be no ideological hegemony but, rather, openness to any ideology, as long as it does not erode moral and political society. What do we define as the "morality"? I know, morality, or morals, is generally attributed to religion. This is how it is evaluated: when we think of morals, we automatically think of religion, but if we go a step further back to the earlier times before religion, we see that morals are established by society itself. At the beginning, as we have said, women were the leaders or guides of society, and the morality in place did not leave society open to the theft of its surplus product or to the creation of hierarchy and negative authority. There is positive authority, and there is negative authority. Positive authority does not allow you to lay claim to something just because you did something good. You don't get to live off of that. Negative authority arises when you begin to construct and build your domination or monopoly over society, because you did something. Therefore, every viewpoint and belief has the right to be expressed, as long as the positive aspects of society are not eroded.

Representative democracy in capitalism strips away the political. We vote every so often, and that is the limit of our politics. In the kind of society that we are talking about politics takes place in meeting rooms. Some of you were here on the first day when we talked about how meetings are where transformation occurs. This is how meetings must be used, so that they are not just bureaucratic spaces for banal decision-making. On the contrary, let me tell you something I have heard. In Rojava, a woman was asked how much she loved her husband or her partner. She answered, "I love him like the Apoists love their meetings." This shows how numerous these meetings are and how important they really are. As we said, we need to talk and articulate if we are to decide how we want to build things and how we want to live. Our purpose in life is not to work and make money. So we need to question the purpose of life and living in line with that.

That is why democratic confederalism has these principles on an even larger scale. Democratic autonomy is even more important, because it's more grassroots; it opens up space for those different segments of the society to organize themselves and, at the same time, is the way to establish a relationship or reconciliation with the nation-states. As such, it plays two very important roles. It is defined as democratic governance, or the authority of the people based on radical democracy. It is not representative, and it aims for direct involvement and participation of the grassroots organized in the way that I have described—in production, by controlling the means of production, in education, in social relations and decision-making mechanisms, and for self-defense.

So what does self-government look like? You will have communes and councils from the village level up. In suburbs, in neighborhoods, as well as in municipalities. Öcalan was very fond of Bookchin for this idea in particular—but not just that. The book that we will be publishing with PM Press talks a bit about organic society.[4] There are parallels between Öcalan's moral and political society and Bookchin's organic society. He is fond of some of Bookchin's books, especially the one that addressed libertarian municipalism.[5] At the time, he proposed that all Kurdish municipalities read the book. He said, "Everyone has to read this." I guess this is when most of Kurdish society first heard of Bookchin. Everything we are talking about: municipalities, local councils, committees, communes, autonomous movements, numerous other groups, belief communities, etc. and their autonomous organizations together constitute this self-governance.

I will now turn my attention to the political dimension of the democratic nation.

For a reconciliation to occur between nation-states and democratic autonomies, nation-states have to acknowledge democratic autonomy. Otherwise, self-defense mechanisms will play an even greater role. I don't know how much you followed the talks between the PKK and Öcalan and the Turkish state. The Turkish state kept saying that the PKK would have to disarm before an agreement could be reached. If you ever get the chance, read the book *The Road Map to Negotiations*,[6] which we published in English. It was the document that was the basis for the talks Öcalan and the PKK had with the Turkish state. Of course, during these talks, the movement made clear that given the almost one hundred years of attacks on the community, the self-defense mechanisms of the community had to be accepted. Because the Kurdish freedom movement refused to disarm before reaching an agreement, the talks broke down, and the Turkish state's genocidal intent toward the Kurdish people was once again made clear.

How do we define the democratic nation? To implement something, you have to have the appropriate ideological principles and philosophy, as well as the necessary political mechanisms. This is why we talked a little bit about *jineolojî*. We talked about why and how positivism, rationalism, etc. are critiqued. What the current form of democratic nation is, how it is defined, how to avoid it becoming a state tool, and what the precautions taken are. The democratic nation is not meant to define the Kurdish nation becoming democratic. A new nationhood is being defined, one that does not rest on a state. It is plural. It is defined as ecological and based on women's freedom, as an optimal balance of individual freedom, the communal, and the collective, as people becoming a nation without relying on power, hierarchy, or the state. This is the only way to create a democratic society. Instead of the nation of the state, it's this new meaning given to nation. Since it is described as a mindset, it is very dynamic. It's not about an ethnicity. It's not about a language. It's not about any of that.

The democratic nation is based on consciousness of freedom and on solidarity. Its definition is very, very dynamic, which prevents it from falling into nationalism or making any similar misstep. The political form of the nationalist mindset is the nation-state, and the political form of nations based on freedom and solidarity is defined as democratic autonomy. In that sense, the homeland is not above everything else; a free society is above everything else. This is more meaningful, as it is not about the sacredness of the homeland but about enchantment and the meaning of life as the philosophical basis for those ideas. Differences are seen as richness and wealth instead of as something to be reckoned with or to be frightened by. Furthermore, governance, even in the form of self-governance, is not to be turned into something sacred either. Governance should be very simple and geared toward making life simpler and serving the needs of life and the day-to-day running of life. This model aims to democratize social relations between peoples, between women and men, between youth and women, and between the elderly and the youth, and so forth, because the state's nationhood model has actually fragmented these social relations. It has created numerous privileges, with one oppressing another, with one above and one below, and so on. Thus, the aim is to also democratize social relations.

There are ten principles that describe the democratic nation. You can see these in Abdullah Öcalan's pamphlet titled *Democratic Nation*.[7] This pamphlet is a compilation from Öcalan's various books. All ten dimensions are extremely important. Social life is very important. Women's freedom is very important. The relationship between women and men and how they are defined is also very important. So is overcoming the binary of life and death. All of this is open for discussion, which leaves the concept and definition of democratic nation open. It is not a finalized definition but an open and dynamic expression and definition that is continuously discussed and implemented. It includes economic autonomy. It includes a discussion and critique of law and the legal system. We talked a little bit about that yesterday, about how the autonomous women's movement was looking into cases, especially where women were involved, and making decisions in these cases. We also talked about culture. This is also important, because the culture of society has also been significantly eroded to legitimize theft, oppression, and colonization. We simply look the other way. It has become increasingly acceptable. Reviving the culture is also a dimension of the democratic nation. We also talked about self-defense and about diplomacy. Diplomacy should not be understood as it currently is, as a process used by states to prepare before launching a war. Earlier it was part of the process of peacemaking, genuine peacemaking. Therefore, Öcalan is now talking about a new form of diplomacy between peoples that would ensure that all of the struggles being waged in different dimensions around the world come together to discuss how to advance their struggles and how to universally connect their struggles and their undertakings.

The tenth principle is, of course, particularly for activists and revolutionaries. The tenth dimension is to be a seeker of truth. To actually understand what has been going on for the last five to six thousand years. To deconstruct everything, so that we know in fine detail what to do, because we have all been made to believe in a life free of problems. Hollywood movies play a particular role in this. There is a problem and you combat it, and the resulting happiness resembles death. You are back at where you started. Nothing happens. No new problems arise. Öcalan is saying, let's look at this somewhat differently. We encounter problems, and we resolve them. This is not a burden. This is not something to be frightened about. It is something to be confronted, and, in that confrontation, we must grasp that very moment to think and to do and to do and to think.

Maybe, in that moment of confrontation, we can transform both ourselves and, with us, the community. Transformation. This is also how we said burnout can be combatted. The best

way to combat burnout is to make sure that you are enjoy-
ing yourself, because you are also transforming yourself and
advancing and creating your own hope as you go. It not like
factory work or the work you do for money. That is where
burnout actually occurs.

The tenth dimension of the democratic nation actually
addresses this. This dimension is for everybody, because the
more we seek the truth of ourselves, of our community, of our
relations with one another, the more we find we are doing
that for reasons other than profit or moneymaking or career-
building or whatever. Whatever we do in this system, we do
to improve life and living and, therefore, to visualize another
way of living. Then we will be able to better pursue the other
nine dimensions. We have to start where it matters, and this is
where the Kurdish freedom movement has started: in personal
life. They didn't start just by critiquing the state or this and
that. They critiqued the family. They critiqued the making and
the raising of children and the relationship between men and
women. When you make personal change, it has a ripple effect.
It reinstates hope that things can change, because you have
changed. These days, they force us not to change. This is a bit
upside down. They don't want us to change the overall system,
so we make cosmetic changes to ourselves—to our hair, to our
clothes, to our eating habits. To some degree, these changes
can be important, of course, but if they are keeping us from
addressing larger change, that is a huge problem.

Today, we are going through an extremely important historical moment in human history. Problems have been increasingly accumulating and becoming more concentrated. We are
seeing this in the form of terrible wars, in the Middle East and
in different ways around the world. In Africa, people are dying
of hunger, and this is inflicted. In the Middle East, its physical death from weapons, from arms, through the incitement
of religionism, nationalism, and sexism, by trying to create a
much more fascistic society. We know that this is also inflicted,

because the Rojava revolution and the coexistence of peoples shows us that this is not inherent, that it is imposed. In Latin America and elsewhere in the Americas, we are seeing opposition to recolonization of the lands and to the pillaging of the people's natural resources, in short, opposition to land grabbing, whether by the drug cartels or otherwise. Of course, we also have the severe femicides in Mexico and elsewhere in the Americas.

It is not all bad. I keep saying this. It looks bad, but it is not all bad, because all this violence is used with one single intention: to prevent people from seizing the moment and making change. Today, what we are facing is the collapsing of capitalism, the structural crisis of capitalism. I said this on the first day, and I want to repeat it today as we wrap things up: this structural crisis didn't just arise on its own. Our struggles, no matter where we are, brought this about. Therefore, the status quo of both world wars is no longer tenable. We are seeing that in the way that these states are disregarding this status quo—not only global capital, which the US represents, along with the national capitals of Turkey, Iran, and others. We are seeing that nobody is adhering to the institutions that were born out of the two world wars. So why would the colonized, the workers, the women be the protectors of the status quo that oppressed them and that they were actually struggling to destroy? This is why Öcalan calls this era the Age of Hope.

Humanity now knows a lot more about what happened in the past, how it happened, and how we can stop it from being perpetuated. On the basis of this knowledge, Öcalan proposes a paradigm that is based on moral and political society: democratic confederalism and democratic autonomy to create an alternative way of life that is not statist. Today, Kurds are actually struggling within the grip of the genocidal efforts of all of the states and imperialist forces. Neither the US nor Russia care what happens to peoples. They don't care about the Kurds, nor do they care about the Arabs or the Turks. They don't care

about you. They don't care about anyone! The freedom movement is very much aware of this. This is where the goals and
intentions overlap.

On the one hand, the traditional nation-states in the
Middle East, including Iran and Turkey, are working together
and are definitely insisting on the old world order. They see
the Kurdish resistance and revolution as a threat to this. But
the imperial powers also see this resistance and revolution
as a threat, because this is the moment when you can actually
do something new, say: democratic confederalism. This is why
they are doing everything they can to co-opt and appropriate
the revolution in Rojava and, thus, the genocidal grip squeez-
ing the Kurdish people just gets tighter. But the Kurdish people
have proven themselves to be resilient time and again. Today,
with people around the world joining the Kurdish people,
networking with them, supporting them, and expressing solidarity—something that needs to continue to grow, of course—
there is substantial hope that this age, the twenty-first century,
can become the age of freedom for women and for peoples.

Q: *You say that the whole society depends on the confederation at
the local original divisions, and I am wondering: Who is looking
into the whole picture? Let's say this group here is deciding to do
something, and that group is deciding to do something, but they
are doing the same thing, and what's missing is nobody is taking
care of it. Here, all they know is to grow wheat, so they grow wheat.
There, all they know is to grow wheat, so they grow wheat. But
then they need corn or something else. Who is looking at the big
picture to teach them how to do something else or to give them
the tools? Also, for example, some group here is not doing as well,
because they are not near decent water resources or whatnot, so
they are not producing enough to meet their needs. What kind
of system is there to make sure that everybody has their needs
met, and who decides what is most important? Maybe a group
of women say, "I need hair dye," but then the kids need diapers or*

whatnot. Resources are limited. Who gets to decide what's most important, and what kind of mechanisms are there to come up with some solutions to solve the problems? And who owns the production tools? Who is overlooking the big picture, and how are they managing it?

Havin: It's highly mixed at the moment, of course. We are talking about the ideal. It is highly mixed over there, at the moment. We talked about societycide. I have to say that Rojava is one of the places where the most intense state hegemony and control was experienced. Yesterday or the day before, we talked a little bit about the fact that society couldn't even decide what to harvest, what to do, whether to plant strawberries or not. They couldn't decide that. What is being attempted over there at the moment is to get everybody at the very different levels organized. This is at the village level. What happens on the regional level of the Northern Syrian Federation is that cantons, areas, the women's movement, and the education movement—everybody sends their delegates there to decide on the far-reaching questions that await resolution. When I was there, they were talking about thread, thread for sewing. The factory wasn't running. There was a dire need to produce different types of thread. They decided how to address this at the level of the federation at these meetings with all the different delegates. Or, let's say, one canton needs something. In the canton of Afrin, before the Turkish occupation, they had soap, olive oil, and olives. The canton of Cizre had the wheat and so forth. They would discuss trade and send their products to one another using these mechanisms.

There is another aspect as well, and that is that, at the moment, there is a war economy in place. Rojava is under dire threat, and not just from one power but from several. We are seeing a daily attempt to change the balance of power, so that should the Syrian regime and the North Syrian Federation find themselves at the negotiating table, the latter no longer has a particularly strong hand.

There are lots of politics at play on that front as well. I would say that nobody is sitting centrally and saying, "You've got to give cotton to whoever." What happens is that the delegates from all these different places come to the meetings of the North Syrian Federation, and the decisions that concern the more regional levels are made there, whereas problems at the local levels are resolved at the local level. They don't require the intervention of the regional level. So it depends on the dimension of the problem. That is also true for self-defense. At the local level, security is more grounded in and tied to the local decision-making structures, but on a more regional level, it is a little bit different.

Q: *To press this question a little bit further, I'd like to stay with the same theme before we move on. I'm wondering if you could compare and contrast this decision-making structure, this organizational structure you are talking about, with the Zapatista caracol structure that may be the last momentous thing that the global anarchist movement looked at and said, "Ah, look at this decision-making structure, this organizational structure that's working in this particular place." With these five caracoles and the breakdown into municipalities and then into villages, and villages making decisions at the local level and then sending immediately recallable delegates who are accountable to the decisions of their villages and accountable at the municipal level, and who, when consensus is reached, then bring it back to their villages. Then each village agrees, "Yeah that's the position we delegated you to represent." In that case, the decision stands, and it goes to the caracole level. But if one village says, "No, that's not the position we delegated you to represent," then it comes back again. Maybe also comparing and contrasting it to sociocracy: this governance structure that is proposed in a lot of places, which is also similar. These circles that have two double links where one person is more accountable to the outer circle and one person is more accountable to the inner circle facilitate communication that is* *built from the bottom up toward consensus. Could you compare and contrast this organizational structure you are speaking the one I've just described to provide some nuance?*

Havin: It's a little bit more complex than that, I think. As I explained, it's not just about decision-making in the village and the neighborhood or the councils. It is also about the organization of the internally oppressed, women, for example. As far as I know, there are no separate and autonomous structured women's organizations within the Zapatista communities—or the youth, for example. So you have multilayered autonomous organizations that then come together at the village or regional level or in the city or at the neighborhood level. What they are doing is continuously and actively trying to combat the formation of power centers. In the village, there could be a lot of patriarchal men, so the women can't really express themselves. Maybe one individual will be crazy enough to say, "Go away! This is the right thing." But you are addressing that on an organized level. This is what I meant about invigorating every instance of society. You're not just leaving society to its traditional values, right? Those traditional values are not all really values of freedom and are not open to freedom. Don't forget, it's not just about capitalism. It's about feudalism and patriarchy in general—and the youth also, in this context. The youth are also autonomously organized, and young women are also organized within the youth to combat the young men's controlling and oppressive behaviors. Take education or cooperatives or health. All of these things that have been stripped away from the community you are reorganizing. You bring people together. I usually joke that the only ones that don't need to be organized are the men, because they are already organized. The freedom movement is trying to break that up. This is why, if you go to Rojava, you will see that every unit or movement has its autonomous education. Women's autonomous structures have education of their own. There is education within the economy committees. There is education within education movement. Really! There is movement to recover and discover. We went to visit the center where the curriculum is drawn up in Rojava. I'm extremely interested in education.

We have these conferences in Hamburg. We have a network called "Network for an Alternative Quest." The overall title of the conferences is "Challenging Capitalist Modernity," and every two years we have a subtitle depending on what we are discussing. At the last conference, we discussed how to deepen our discussions, how to map out our approach to deconstructing the enslavement institutions and tools and creating new ones on a universal level, on a global level. It is not only capital that has to be global, right? The freedom struggle has to be global in its thinking as well. One of the ideas was to establish a working group on education and curriculum. We went to Rojava with some of the people who were involved with this working group. There, we went and visited the center for curriculum. It was a very interesting experience. It was structured such that the Assyrian team drew up the curriculum for Assyrian schools, the Arab team or committee prepared the curriculum for the Arab community, and the Kurdish team addressed the Kurdish curriculum. They too, in keeping with the model we have been talking about here, had a women's committee at the curriculum center. All of this, because they were being very careful that the curricula in the three different languages, with their distinct cultural concepts, did not retain nationalism, sexism, age discrimination, etc. There were about 160 people living there and doing this work. They were continuously updating the curricula. As they worked, there were criticisms directed to them: "Oh, yeah, a bit of nationalism seeped in here, and here is a bit of sexism." Nobody is saying that the outcome is perfect. On the contrary, while they don't want it to become a yoyo, they do want to keep the process open and directed toward freedom. As the discussions develop and change, they want to make sure the curricula are also changing to keep up.

I found it interesting that they were all living together while working on the curricula together. I would say this is a small part of the difference. Because hierarchies can be established using very strange ways and means—even small and simple things. For example, if you have some kind of authority over the supply chain, you can become a bloody god! Therefore, they are very careful to plot or map out possible areas of monopolization. This is why education is independent: to make sure that knowledge does not become capital, that it's not produced for profit. This is the problem with capitalist knowledge production, isn't it? Or with social sciences or whatever. Knowledge production is funded by capitalists so that it benefits them and does not really expose them, so we are thankful to intellectuals who have actually produced knowledge for all, exposing what has been going on. There are lots of different intellectuals who have done this, both living and no longer living, from Immanuel Wallerstein to Andre Gunder Frank, from Fernand Braudel to David Graeber, from Michel Foucault to John Holloway. There are so many people who have worked in these centers. Maria Mies: very important. Silvia Federici and many other women and men too numerous to even begin mentioning. This would be, I would say, the difference. Additionally, because there is learning and reinforcement of what is being learned through making, and they expose new knowledge through making. I guess this is how the Kurdish freedom movement also transformed itself. They made, and they thought, "Wait a minute. What we have done is not how we had thought." So they reevaluated that and redid it. This is the end product for now. Nobody is making this sacred either. It is open to discussion. It is open to criticism. It is open to reenvisioning.

Q: *I have a quick question. Is it possible for us to visit Rojava? If so, how do we do that?*
Havin: [Laughs] I think it is possible. A lot of people have done it and continue to do it. There are flights that can be taken to

neighboring countries, and there are border crossings then to Rojava. But, of course, it's not just about going there. It's important, of course, but I think the defense of Rojava is also important. If we are looking at internationalism and solidarity, we should look at it in more ways than one. To be able to take that moment wherever we are and to organize to that end is also very important. This is also another form of solidarity and support. To make sure that we also uncover the truth wherever we are and organize on that basis. Rojava didn't come out of nowhere. It was stewing for a while.

I think that I mentioned on the first night that in 1979, when Öcalan and some of his friends escaped the 1980 military coup, leaving before it happened, they first went to Kobanî, because that's the border town with Turkey. They began organizing from there. There is an organizational process that has been going on for forty-five years, just waiting for the moment. In those early days, there was a lot of criticism of the movement: "What are you doing in Syrian Kurdistan? It's all about Northern Kurdistan," etc. But, you know, they were organizing the people and making them aware. Women were being organized, the youth was being organized, the society as a whole was being organized, and when the moment arrived it could be seized because of that organizing among the people for so many years. It didn't just occur on the spur of the moment. It was deep-rooted. This is very important. It may not seem to have an effect immediately, but becoming aware, meeting under the same roof, discussing, making decisions, and uncovering reality are extremely important. Organization or organizing is a matter of persistence and takes years. So, yes, please go there but not just that.

Q: *I'm interested in what you were talking about earlier, for example, the people who are making education and stuff. Obviously, there are still going to be people who are corrupt, who want to do things that are not in line with the principles*

*of democratic confederalism. What is in place to hold people
accountable when they are in positions with more power?*
Havin: Actually, it was so great to see all these discussions
in Rojava, and specifically, for example, at Rojava University.
They were having all these discussions about how to get out of
that teacher/student binary and so forth and how to make it
more dynamic so that, as well as having knowledge, the teachers or professors or whatever also acquired knowledge, to
prevent them from becoming dogmatic. There is the student
council. Again, there is the Jineoloji Department as well as the
course on jineoloji being a prerequisite for both teachers and
for students, to break the patriarchal mindset and this scientism of science.

We also saw that this is not just about a small number
of sympathizers. It is a six-million-person geographical area,
and they are not all pro–democratic confederalism or pro–
women's movement or pro–women's freedom or pro–alternative education. So if you don't want to become a new Stalin,
you have to convince people. So the discussion circulated
around the fact that the Kurds, most of whom did not have citizenship, had always dreamed of going to university, but most
of them couldn't, because you couldn't go to the university if
you weren't a citizen. Some of the professors and the students
were actively seeking to make sure that Rojava University's
diploma was recognized by states in general and by the Syrian
state in particular. So there was a whole mix of discussions
there. On the one hand, this and, on the other hand, something
very radical like jineolojî. There is a Jineolojî Faculty being
built there as well. So there are intermediate steps. Rojava
University is between moments. It is both a traditional university and a radical alternative education institute, represented
by the Mesopotamia Academy, which offers a radical alternative education. Therefore, it involves a lot of convincing and
discussions, both internal and external, with democratic and
radical people, those who have been sympathetic to these ideas

and those who have not been previously been. This is why I said it is always dynamic, because what they are trying to do is to bring everybody together, keep a pace of moving forward together and to cut the arms off the octopus at the same time. If you do this with a top-down command structure, then there is the danger that you will become like Stalin. But if you do not struggle with it, then there is the danger that you will allow the traditional, hegemonic forces or reactionary forces from within society to once again take control. Ideally or abstractly thinking about these things and putting them into practice are actually totally different. One must be aware of the dynamics of society or how easy it is to fall into either one or the other error, and your safeguard against that is all of these different autonomous organizations that we have been talking about: these layers, these overlapping organizations.

In that education movement, you also have, for example, women involved who also take part in the structures of the autonomous women's movement, among other things. This helps to make sure that everyone moves and advances forward together, in a rhythm. It's not enough that I'm very clever and so very free, because the whole society has to move in that direction as one. That is the sense in which they are trying to dampen elitism, a situation where one section moves ahead, but everybody else is unable to follow. This is also a very important dynamic that must be preserved.

Q: *I'm intrigued by these books you keep mentioning. Is there some way that we can get these books when they arrive? Or, just in general, what are a couple of books that you recommend that we read?*

Havin: You can have a look at ocalanbooks.com. PDFs of the pamphlets that I have been talking about are available there and are free to download. I haven't discussed this with PM Press, but, hopefully, when our boxes arrive, we'll be able to arrange for PM Press to distribute them. But you can get the books from ocalanbooks.com, or you can write to us. Basically, all of the books there are important. It may also be important that you read the people that Öcalan mentions. Because Öcalan and the Kurdish freedom movement have also learned a lot from all the people and movements mentioned, as well as from their own experiences, which I talked about in detail on the first day. Their heritage is the struggle of women and peoples and the working class all over the world, as well as the intellectuals who have been seeking and exposing the truth. It is a combination of all of this.

Q: *What is the best practice, in your experience in Rojava, for organizing community police, an alternative to the police, a different way of organizing safety within the community? Could you tell us a little bit more about that?*

Havin: At the moment, things are extreme in Rojava. There are continuous interventions into both society's fabric in different ways and physical attacks on society, including car bombs, etc. There is the *asayish*, which is internal security. It is made up of local civilians who have basic training and the responsibility for maintaining security at the local level. They also, of course, have connections to and are participants in local organizations, including communes, councils, and cooperatives. There are women who are part of the asayish, who also are part of the autonomous women's movement. So the same kind of organizational structures are in place whether we're dealing with education or the asayish—no matter what it is. In this way, you intentionally avoid the asayish becoming a profession in the hands of a group of people. As a result, you are not militarizing society but are, instead, demilitarizing self-defense. This is what they are trying to do. The idea is to enable the people to defend themselves without militarization. I think that this is an important aspect, and it is not in a way that makes them afraid of each other. Especially under the current conditions in Rojava, it is very important that people know how to defend themselves when the time comes. In the Middle East right now, of course, that is something people must always be ready for. That is why this is extremely important, for example, in the case of the Yazidi people, or even the Assyrians, since they are also a minority in the area. This allows them to avoid being at the mercy of some other self-defense force. This is important in that sense. Self-defense or the asayish do not exist to protect a given monopoly or some profits but to protect the community itself.

Q: *I heard another speaker say that they were a Kurdish nationalist, up until the moment that a Kurdish state was created, then they would seek to immediately dismantle the state. I'm curious, would you see the Kurdish state as a welcome step along the way to democratic confederalism or as counterproductive to the movement?*

Havin: We talked about that on the two previous nights. The freedom movement criticizes the socialist practice of looking to the state, the idea that you first seize the state, and then you dismantle it. This is not just about Kurdish nationalism. This is how the left generally proceeded, for example, the national liberation movements, the dictatorship of the proletariat, etc. But this has only led these practices straight back to capitalism. Therefore, the Kurdish freedom movement is aware of this. For example, in Iraqi Kurdistan, the project is to achieve a nation-state. But in fact, when you look at it in detail and from close-up, that process doesn't actually look like nation-building. The result isn't a Kurdistan Regional Government (KRG), as they claim. It is a lot like a province shared by Turkey and Iran. It's doesn't even reach the level of a state. I'm not saying this would be positive thing. All I'm saying is that the state tool is a tool that absorbs its user. I refer to it as "the victim becoming the perpetrator." The tool itself cannot be our savior, and it can't be used to achieve liberation. So, no, it's not a welcome step. We talked about it as a step that nationalizes, that turns the people into nationalists. Therefore, no, it is not at all seen as a tool in the sense you are asking about.

Q: *I would like to understand the economic aspects of this movement. How does this movement overcome the capitalist economic system? For example, how and by whom would wages be determined? How is the system going to prevent capital accumulation?*
Havin: There are certain principles, of course. We discussed the fact that production is not based on making a profit. No monopolization of any sort is permitted. Property is not completely rejected, but property by accumulation is rejected. In that sense, monopolization of property is rejected. At the moment, it's a mixed bag. It cannot be said that "they are there." That's not the case. The idea is, through these multidimensional organizations, to aim for a system without wages. The idea is to overcome the wage system. The idea is not to work for profit or money or whatever. We are saying that how life is envisioned must be completely different. They work enough to meet their needs and no more than that, not beyond that. These are the basic principles. Thus, the aim is to eliminate exploitation, monopolization, and profit-making at every possible level and in every dimension. The market is not totally disregarded, but its monopolization aspects are. And then there is the critique of the production of commodities. The basic necessities like food, housing, and health care should not be traded as commodities for profit, but are something that society should provide for its members. This is a process of continuous development. There isn't, as yet, an economic policy that you can see, even if you went to Rojava, because that is still in the making, on the basis of the principles I just outlined.

Q: *I understand that there is a sort of hierarchy to societies, whether it comes from institutions or even from patriarchy. If you strip all of that away, and you are left with just humans, there is still that ego and the way that we are flawed. How do you* *ensure that that doesn't affect this kind of society, such that smart people are able to manipulate others and are able to advance their agendas?*

Havin: It's a fair question, and, of course, none of what I'm talking about will work if people do not strive and struggle for it to work. Let's say we are in an autonomous women's movement meeting. If we allow hierarchies to be established there, then having an autonomous women's movement will not really mean much. Or let's say we have a meeting of autonomous women, autonomous youth, education, whatever, everyone else, and there is a discussion. If you're not exposing problem areas or issues by critiquing them, waging a struggle against them, and/or changing and transforming yourself—struggling with yourself for transformation—and are not making the changes that you need to, then none of this will work. It's not only about the mechanisms that you put in place; it's about how much you actually make the attempt and struggle to make it work, instead of just accepting things as they are. Patriarchal characteristics are extremely vicious and when they see a vacuum and feel they can fill that vacuum, they will recur and impose themselves once again. All the things that I've been talking about are safeguards, but the real and true safeguard is how you wage the struggle within as well. Sometimes this is difficult. You know why it's difficult? Because if I criticize you, you're going to criticize me, so I don't criticize you, so that I can remain just as I am. Some people may be smarter, but maybe I draw well, and you don't. We all have something. This is something that hierarchy generates; it is as if one talent is better than another. We stopped to consider how everything together creates the perfect picture: I can sing, you can do something else. Maybe we have been overly compartmentalized. Maybe we all have the ability to do more than one thing.

We don't have to look very far. Just look back at ancient Greece, and you will see that people did more than one thing. Pythagoras was more than just a mathematician; he was also a very good painter. But, today, under capitalism, we increasingly only do one thing. Therefore, we don't see the whole picture. Everybody just sees what they are doing. We lose the enchantment of wholeness. I was trained as an engineer, and the way that I was taught to think is very different. It was based in mathematics and the idea that you can engineer society, that you can impose things on society. As if society has no spirit and soul of its own. More often than not, we also ignore the reality of action and reaction, how when something bumps into something else it creates a completely new synthesis of the two elements that constitute it. You get a completely bizarre and different thing. Öcalan wants to pave a path to these possibilities. Öcalan is trying to construct a social science based on quantum mechanics. I can't even begin to describe it. You have to read it.

Q: *I have a question about the practice of* tekmil. *The critique and self-critique in the self-defense forces. I have never really gotten a straight answer about how long that's been going on. I see the practical benefit of it but what is the theoretical concept and idea behind it.*

Havin: It's been going on for a very long time. The tipping point for directing critique or self-critique inward began as early as 1983, but even more so after 1986. Because there were bottlenecks. Theoretically, things were fine, but in practice when discussing something and finally saying, "Okay, we are going to go and do this," if there are ten people there would be ten different approaches to implementation. Therefore, they began critique and self-critique, which is a bit more profound and long-term. Over the course of a year or two, anyone could give a pretty profound self-critique as to why a particular practice has been what it is. This is not like a confession in a church. It's about comparing your praxis with the paradigm that you say you think is best for attaining freedom. You compare yourself against that paradigm, and you say, "Okay, these are my feudal traits." They—some attributes and characteristic—have almost become genetic. We are subjected to the same schooling, education, media, films, poetry—even the colors we like are dictated to us. Each and every year this changes. Therefore, critique and self-critique is more profound.

Tekmil is not as profound. Tekmil is more a day-to-day running of things, you may think of it as feedback. For example, they may do a tekmil after this seminar. What would happen if this was an education session of the movement is that they would say, "Okay, the education is finished. Now we will have a tekmil." People would evaluate how the education committee handled the day. Let's say I was the one who did the presentation. I would learn from what I did, from what my presentation bumped up against, what it failed to achieve, etc. Or the tekmil could be about the day. Let's say we all had responsibilities. Then I could criticize you. I could say, "You were supposed to bring the papers." It's not about bringing the papers, obviously, but about responsibility. If you were responsible for self-defense or the security of the area, but you didn't do it properly, and somebody else was responsible for the kitchen. You prevent the development of much graver mistakes by doing a five-minute evaluation, not a very long one, just a very superficial one to prevent it from happening again the next day, because if a week went by and none of the tasks were done properly, that would result in even graver problems, so you try to minimize the problems.

Of course, everything except one thing is open to discussion. Women's freedom is not open to discussion. This is a consensus. If you're at a council meeting, freedom of speech or democracy can't be used to say, "I'm against these autonomous women's movements." That doesn't happen. Things like that don't happen.

Tekmil and critique and self-critique: I can distinguish between the two to some degree as follows. Tekmil stops people from gossiping, or, rather, from complaining. It provides room for people to talk about daily issues and for up-front discussions. It stops problems from worsening. It prevents misunderstandings. It ensures duties and responsibilities are properly addressed.

Notes

1   Fernand Braudel, *Civilization and Capitalism, Volume III: The Perspective of the World* (New York: Harper & Row, 1984), 295.

2   Abdullah Öcalan, *The Sociology of Freedom: Manifesto of the Democratic Civilization*, vol. 3 (Oakland, PM Press, 2020), 209–10.

3   Georg Wilhelm Friedrich Hegel, *The Philosophy of Right* (Oxford: Clarendon Press, 1952 [1821]), 233.

4   Abdullah Öcalan, *Beyond State, Power, and Violence* (Oakland: PM Press, 2021).

5   Murray Bookchin: *Urbanization without Cities: The Rise and Decline of Citizenship* (Montreal: Black Rose Books, 1992).

6   Abdullah Öcalan, *Prison Writings III: The Road Map to Negotiations* (Cologne: International Initiative, 2012).

7   Abdullah Öcalan, *Democratic Nation* (Cologne: International Initiative Edition, 2016), accessed December 14, 2020, http://ocalanbooks.com/downloads/democratic-nation.pdf.

Havin Guneser Interviewed
by Sasha Lilley

Sasha: *Kurds, as a group, preceded the rise of the nation-state. Can you start by telling us who the Kurds are and outlining the trajectory of the Kurdish struggle from the end of the Persian and Ottoman Empires, through the two world wars?*

Havin: Kurds are indigenous to the Mesopotamia area. Over time, especially with the intervention of the capitalist world system into the Middle East, states, empires, and dynasties came to an end, and the Kurds were basically divided between the various Persian Shia empires and the Ottoman Empire. At the time, these empires and dynasties were not based on a single ethnicity, and, despite the fact that they were Islamic, and in spite of the oppression, suppression, and exploitation, there was a little bit of maneuvering room. Don't get me wrong. I'm not saying that those empires were the best possible option—to the contrary. The thing was that the empires were not based on a dominant ethnicity, therefore, there were a lot of different autonomous peoples living within those former states. Kurds were one of the people in those empires. There were others, of course: Armenians, Assyrians, and many other people that are no longer exist in our world.

When the nation-state was introduced into the Middle East, it was actually as destructive as it had been everywhere else, because it based the state on a single language, a single ethnicity, a dominant ethnicity, or a dominant religion, thereby excluding and attempting to assimilate other people, and if that didn't work, eliminating these languages and people. A language that is not used in education is a dying language. What I'm trying to say here is that even in states where we no longer stop to think about whether or not any other peoples have ever lived there, the situation is the same. This has, however, had more devastating effects in the area we know as the cradle of civilization. It wasn't particularly easy to assimilate peoples with such deep roots stretching back into the depths of history, making genocide the go-to solution. The Armenians experienced genocide, and so did the Assyrians and the Kurds. The Kurds have experienced genocides and massacres in all four parts of occupied Kurdistan.

There was nowhere for the Kurds to go, because the world system has been organized on the basis of the existing nation-states. Therefore, the UN, for example, will not look into the issues raised by Kurds, unless, of course, they could find a powerful state to back them, and this has never happened. Even if they had their own problems and contradictions, when it comes to the Kurdish issue, the four states concerned, Iran, Iraq, Syria, and Turkey, concur and have agreed on an approach to suppressing the Kurds. They have always been able to agree that the suppression of the Kurds is necessary, and that continues today.

Sasha: *You mentioned that the Turkish state perceived the Kurds as isolated in a section of the region in the 1970s and into the 1980s and that the oppression of the Kurds was intensified. Can you tell us about the emergence of the Kurdish freedom movement in Turkey at that time? In what context did that take place, and what kind of ideology did it have?*

Havin: It was an extremely difficult time, especially by the 1970s, although there was the huge 1968 wave of revolutionary soul and spirit around the world that revitalized the left, which, of course, had an influence and effect in the Middle East, including in Turkey. But when you look at what was happening to the Kurds, you see that the Turkish state thought that it had successfully rid itself of that problem, after committing genocide to eliminate the Assyrian and Armenian problems and having gotten rid of the Greeks and the Pontus people. All these different peoples who once coexisted side by side were either sent to Greece or completely assimilated, either forcibly or by embracing opportunities to shed their identity. They used a number of different techniques for this: carrots and sticks and so forth. In 1970s, the Turkish left was very, very strong, and some of its leaders were, in fact, extremely good on the Kurdish issue. Deniz Gezmiş, for example, said, "Both peoples should coexist peacefully and with dignity" and other things of that sort.

There was a major military coup in Turkey in 1971. This military coup was an intervention against the Turkish left. It was at this point that the initial PKK grouping, led by Abdullah Öcalan, first appeared on the scene. They were looking for ways to alleviate the problems of the Kurdish people, because coming from Kurdish families and being poor, they knew what the Kurds were facing on a daily basis. In fact, Öcalan and couple of his friends were trying to determine how to proceed and what to do, given that the military coup of 1971 was, as I said, an intervention against the Turkish left and had resulted in left-wing nationalism.

Sasha: *Do you mean the left moved rightward?*
Havin: Yes, that's right. And, therefore, all these leaders who had a different view on these questions were either executed or killed in street shootouts, while others moved further to the right. As I said, all of this was happening at the same time as Abdullah Öcalan and his friends were discussing and attempting to determine what to do next. They soon realized that the approach of the next generation of leaders to the question was: "Okay, we'll have the revolution, and then we'll figure out what

to do about the Kurds." This became the line. As a result, there was a shift to the idea of forming an umbrella organization to expose the Kurdish reality, the truth about the Kurds, because this has been obscured by the pincer grip of the state and its oppression.

They were very influenced by the Turkish left, the Vietnamese liberation movement, and the invigorating wave of revolutions in 1968. In 1973, with their first group, they began discussions around the very simple critique that Kurdistan is a colony. This is all they had at the time, but it was very powerful, because the word *colony* was seldom used at the time. The Turkish left rejected describing Kurdistan as a colony, at that point. They said, "Turkey is a colony. How can a colony have a colony?" There were a lot of weird discussions, at the time. Öcalan and the others didn't take the easy way out. They chose an extremely difficult path. Imagine 1978: this was when the founding congress of the PKK was held. It was held in Diyarbakır, in a very poor village, and there they declared themselves a Marxist-Leninist organization. I usually call this a molotov. You have this Kurdishness, which was and still is suppressed in the Middle East, in all four states that encompassed Kurdistan. Nobody was willing to listen to the grievances of the Kurds. On top of that, you had the Cold War. Despite that, they launched a Marxist-Leninist organization, and they did that in a community that had been pushed back into extreme darkness. If you asked the people living there, it is possible that most of them would not even have known what Marxism was at the time. It was a very interesting way forward.

They weren't only Kurds at the beginning either. Even then, it wasn't just an identity issue. It was always a lot more than that. As I said, when you look at the situation of the Kurds and at this one organization, with founding members from all over Turkey and from different classes within Turkey and Kurdistan, pronouncing itself Marxist-Leninist, it was a recipe for an interesting future, and we can now see what this brought the Kurds and everyone else in the Middle East.

Sasha: *The Kurdistan Workers' Party, or PKK, was formed and, in the 1980s, took up arms and saw itself as Marxist-Leninist. Yet the ideology of the Kurdish freedom movement evolved quite significantly over the subsequent decades. What was the course of that evolution? How were the basic premises of Marxist-Leninism, including the seizure of state power, rethought?*

Havin: Things didn't really develop very smoothly. After the formation of the party in 1978... it was formed in November 1978, so at the very end of 1978. Only two years later, in 1980, there was another military coup in Turkey. This coup was actually directed at this Kurdish organization, because it was spreading and gaining a foothold inside the Kurdish community extremely quickly. Öcalan and some of his friends, seeing the military coup coming, had left Turkey toward the end of 1979 to try to escape the full impact. Some were able to leave the country and others not. Those who couldn't were arrested in the aftermath of the military coup. You may have heard about the terrible dungeons run by this military coup and of the thousands of people who were tortured, not only in prisons but also in sport stadiums. It was an attempt to tame the whole society once again. All this accumulation of knowledge and action was to be neutralized through these several instances of military coups, which were supported by the United States of America. On the one hand, you had people resisting in the prisons. On the other hand, you had others who were in Lebanon in the Beqaa Valley trying to form an organization. The armed struggle didn't begin until 1984.

Sasha: *Was that with the Palestine Liberation Organization in the Beqaa Valley?*

Havin: That's right. What happened is that they went and met with the PLO leaders and, at the time, a place was made for all of the revolutionary movements. Any revolutionary movement could go there and have space for education and training, etc. This is what PKK did, but it also did something different. When Israel invaded Lebanon in 1981, it didn't run away. It actually stayed and protected the line so that that the invasion couldn't progress. As a result, some ten members of the PKK were killed by the Israeli army and another ten or so were taken as prisoners of war. I think this is a very important underlying attribute of this Kurdish freedom movement, that it is not only looking to benefit the Kurdish liberation movement. What it was looking for, even during the very early days when nobody had even heard of it—it wanted to side with the truth, with whatever was the right thing for everybody. This strengthened the amity between peoples wherever this movement went. That was one of its most important attributes.

Of course, they would soon realize that the Soviet Union would have nothing to do with them. That was basically due to the agreement between the Soviet Union and the US, parceling the world out between them, basically an agreement that neither of them would actually give way to or support any new movements in the world. So, not only did being a Marxist-Leninist movement have a negative impact at the level of the world order, but the same was true of its relationship with the Soviet Union. I sometimes say that this was a great development, because, at the time, when any left movement began organizing, it always ended up dependent upon and centered around one real socialist country or another, which prevented it from developing independently.

Sasha: *Sure, and this greatly influenced the ideologies of various groups.*
Havin: Exactly. Maybe this was another reason why the PKK always found itself excluded by all standards. The states in Iran, Iraq, Syria, and Turkey would inevitably see it unfavorably. Turkey: that's a certainty, because the party originated in

Turkey. Furthermore, the lack of support from the Soviet Union and other socialist states allowed the rest of the left to take its distance from the PKK as well. This meant that the organization had to think about the issues a lot harder than would have been the case had it been accepted by many of the socialist countries or movements. Today, this continues to linger to a degree. Some people on the left called the PKK nationalist, while others claimed it's orthodox Stalinist. The religious say it is atheist. If you ask a Turkish nationalist, you will be told it is actually an Armenian organization. It's blasphemy in Turkey to call anyone Armenian, racism is that rampant. Everybody has a terrible view of the PKK, because it fits no one's framework.

Those whom this movement reached don't see it that way, of course. And despite the hardships, since the founding of the PKK, the Kurdish people and others—they aren't all necessarily Kurdish—who have come in contact with the organization have become lifelong friends, because they have seen that, going all the way back to 1978, the PKK never approached things dogmatically, nor has it been particularly open to bullying influence or interference from the outside.

Sasha: *At what point did the PKK actually abandon Marxism-Leninism? And how did the ideas of people like Murray Bookchin and Immanuel Wallerstein become important influences?*
Havin: I think it has been a continuous process. There are still many things that Öcalan appreciates about Marxist ideas—maybe not Marxism, but some of the ideas of Marx, and also of Engels and Lenin and others. He is, of course, very critical as well, but this is kind of the underlying thing about both Öcalan and the freedom movement; they engage in an extensive critique, and not only of others but of themselves as well. I think this is key to how they were even able to gradually overcome themselves.

All of these things I'm describing effected how this movement changed. By the mid- to late 1980s, the PKK was already very critical of the Soviet Union. The organization was not concerned with what was happening externally but also about what was happening internally. I think the women who came to the organization were very important agents of change. On a theoretical level, they were talking about equality and freedom for everybody and so forth, and there were plenty of women involved in founding this movement. They were able to see in their own practice that there was a serious question here. As a result, theory and practice developed hand in hand. Öcalan usually calls this, "Think as you do, and do as you think," so that you are able to distinguish new perceptions and new theories and, thus, new implementations.

This very important aspect was accompanied by a far-reaching critique of the Leninist party model, because of its tendency to create status and to centralize power and the hierarchy. If you look back at the analysis in the movement's books and materials, you will see that there was a lot of discussion of that; it is quite clear. Öcalan always says that there was one thing that they didn't really take a position on all that clearly—whether they wanted a state for the Kurds; they didn't actually clarify that. They lacked clarity, because states were the in thing. In all the socialist countries, that was the Marxism bit: you seize the state, and then use it to implement socialism and communism and so on. During its lifetime, the PKK saw that this didn't work. The Soviet Union collapsed. Other real socialist states collapsed. The national liberation movements around the world had formed states, and that went miserably as well.

Of course, feminism also brought a lot of different facts and aspects of the truth to the forefront, influencing how we viewed things. As I said, their own practice also highlighted things that we were lacking. There was a lot of discussion, especially from 1986 to 1998, about all of this, about women, about why even the party itself and the cadres were becoming bureaucratized, etc. Of course, things always happen when the Kurds are in turmoil. Those years were not very comfortable years. Politically, in 1993, the PKK declared its first unilateral cease-fire with Turkey, arguing that the Kurdish question could be resolved within the borders of Turkey. That was also the first step away from Kurds wanting their own state.

Sasha: *Was this the result of having a Kurdistan that spanned four states?*

Havin: Yes, as well as all the things I have been saying about the how the world system is devised and the past struggles and theories about seizing the state. This is the way the PKK actually moved. When it was exposed to something, it took steps to address it, and when it was exposed to things was also when it developed. This is not to say that back in 1978 they already knew everything. I think that is the beauty of it. That is the dynamic of the PKK's dialectic.

Sasha: *You have been describing the evolution of the PKK, which was started in the late 1970s in what is Turkey, and how the ideas evolved away from the notion of seizing state power and the idea that oppressed ethnic group should strive for an autonomous state of its own. Much happened in 1999 when Öcalan was abducted with the help of the CIA and imprisoned. Yet, unlike many movements, the Kurdish freedom movement has actually had an opportunity to put into practice a lot of its ideas under some of the harshest circumstances. I want to ask you about the developments that have taken place, even though I realize we're leaping over both time and geographic location to the remarkable experiment that has taken place in what is Northern Syria, an area that is called the Democratic Federation of Northern Syria, or just referred to as Rojava. What has happened there? How was it established? And what is its relationship to the ideas developed by the PKK that you've been talking about?*

Havin: I think as we leap forward we need to give a little bit of a description of what was actually happening.

In the 1970s, capitalism reached its peak, which also meant the beginning of its decline. In 1998, we saw the beginning of a new set of interventions in the Middle East, and for that to happen any organization that could become an obstacle had to be removed. Even before Afghanistan, Iraq, or whatever, it was Öcalan and the PKK that first had to be removed. What Öcalan slowly recognized, especially when he saw the different states in Europe, and encountered the different imperialisms—including Russia's, because he made a quick trip to Russia—was how these state games are really played. The questions that that had come before, in 1998, addressed exactly these points: power, hierarchy, the state, etc. and the real socialism that was developing in that context. This is when he made his break with the state, recognizing that it was the tool that invalidated all the efforts and sacrifices and the amazing accumulation of knowledge that historical struggles and peoples all over the world have been assembling. He made a clean break, and, once he did, it became crystal clear to him that the new axis had to be based on the freedom of women. He saw that hierarchy developed out of authority, and then power and the state developed out of this hierarchy and authority. He went back to the Sumerians. In our current situation, the nation-state form of capitalism has become so amazingly multidimensional that there is a terrible societycide. We know of genocides and femicides. We know about the huge damage to environment. Now society is at risk, and he calls this societycide.

That brings us to Rojava, and to understand what's going on there, as well as the larger Kurdish freedom movement, one needs to look at what's happening today through these lenses. The movement argues that there is a World War III going on. This World War III is the expression of the need to once again determine who will be the hegemonic force. US hegemony is not as strong as it once was. Capitalism is also in a structural crisis, which presents us with a world system problem. This is where Kurdish freedom movement becomes immensely important. It now overlaps struggles. It's not just about Kurdish identity at this point. The world system that devised its colonization and occupation is collapsing. Thus, it is also about how to live, and so, in the context of this over-lapping, the movement is advancing a proposal of not only resisting but also building. This is the source of the problem in Rojava. Global capital in the hands of the United States of America wants to remain unhindered, but, domestic capital and national capitals are resisting this. So they work together but at the same time there are contradictions.

There is another aspect, and it's our aspect: workers, people like us, women and others. They have all been strug-gling to destroy this order that has been oppressing and sup-pressing them. Now, this is happening. What the Kurds have done in Rojava is to realize this. It's not about protecting the status-quo, so they are not pro-Assad. They said to Assad, "Hey, Assad, if you accept democratization, that's good enough. We don't want a separate state." Of course, that extends to every-one who is in power in the Middle East, but especially in Syria.

Sasha: *How did this experiment in organizing a whole autono-mous region in Rojava start at a point when world powers were vying for dominance in Syria?*
Havin: As I mentioned, global capital represented by the United States of America continued to concentrate its inter-ventions in the Middle East. It tried to change all the rulers in these states, so that the region would be more open to its hegemony. It tried several things, including what we call the Arab Spring. In that case, it tried to alter and instrumentalize the people's aspirations and hopes and so on and ended up with what we're seeing in Egypt and in Turkey. They thought that with the Adalet ve Kalkınma Partisi (Justice and Development Party; AKP) they could broker an Islamic political party that would work in tandem with them and would be useful for them as a model to apply throughout the Middle East. It could have

an Islamic identity but still be pro-US or whatever. We saw how that backfired in Egypt, and they toppled the Freedom and Justice Party, i.e., Muslim Brotherhood, and put Sisi, the current President of Egypt—a former general—and the others back in power. I don't think any of the hegemonic powers in the world actually want peace and stability. Look at Libya, for example. Libya is now being looted by everybody, and nobody is questioning what's happening. It is a done deal. The situation in Afghanistan is so devestating. Iraq is moving very quickly toward breaking up.

In Syria, of course, the role of the Kurds was very important. The Kurds saw that what the hegemonic powers were trying to do in Syria. After seeing what had happened in Egypt, Libya, Tunisia, etc., it was clear that this is not especially beneficial. So they didn't become the soldiers of hegemonic powers. They said no. Then they looked at Assad. They said, "Well, we have no desire to protect you, because you represent our oppression, so no thanks to you too." So what did they do? They said, "Okay, we're not going to attack anybody, but we will defend ourselves. We will focus on living the way we want to live," which is in a democratic, ecological society based on women's freedom that coexists with other peoples and other belief systems. This is why all the other peoples in Northern Syria also have their own self-defense forces, for example, the Assyrians. It's not a matter of the Kurds saying, "Oh, yes, we are the stronger big brother now. We will protect you." No, to the contrary, other communities can develop their own dynamics as well. Of course, there is the principle of coexistence. People have to adhere to this, and it includes women's freedom.

Sasha: *I wonder if you could define democratic confederalism as it is implemented in Rojava. What does that mean?*
Havin: Well, democratic confederalism is a non-state solution. It's not an alternative state; it's an alternative to the state. We are made to believe that life is impossible without a state. The

state hides its true face behind the services that it appears to provide, which, believe me, is very, very little in Syria anyway. But before I come to that, everybody suddenly discovering Kurds in Syria didn't happen during first phase. At that point, everybody was confused. "Who are they? Whose side are they on?" Questions like that. Everybody began to take notice of them when ISIS began practicing what it had been preaching and creating the Islamic State. It gathered momentum with pro-Saddam leftovers, Al-Nusra Front leftovers, and I don't know what other leftovers. They were all organized. Mind you, there are numerous statements that make it clear that at a point when the US and everybody else had been trying to form some kind of an opposition, they played a major role in helping ISIS become what it is.

When did people notice the Kurds? When ISIS was like a tornado, going from city to city and conquering places without resistance. Then they came to the Kurdish areas, and, "bang," they suffered their first strategic loss. Ever since then, they have been losing. Of course, what we saw in the aftermath was that Turkey in particular began to train and reorient ISIS almost solely against the Kurds. What we saw increasingly was the two traditional powers in the Middle East, Iran and Turkey, which are usually in contradiction and conflict, once again becoming partners in crime, to make sure that there is no room for democratization in the Middle East. Syria was pressured, Iraq was pressured, so that Kurds would not in any way be included in shaping the new Middle East. Look at Iran, it severely suppresses all the peoples within the country, executes Kurds in particular but all that may raise their voices against the injustices and yet, because it is "anti-American," it can be supported by some. What I often don't like is that some of the left fall into the trap of just being anti-American, or anti-American imperialism.

Sasha: *Do you mean "the enemy of my enemy is my friend"?*

Havin: Exactly. Because of this, some people just shut their eyes to what was happening in Iran. If you just look at what happened, Iran executed three young men, Kurdish men, again. It attacked Iraqi Kurdistan and killed around forty people who were at a congress, Kurdish activists from Iran who were at an official congress in Iraqi Kurdistan. Turkey invaded Afrin. Turkey also invaded parts of Iraqi Kurdistan, bombing them day and night. All of this violates international agreements. Since when can you carry out bombings in another country, and it's okay? It's okay both because it's World War III, and because the new status-quo is not yet in place. That is scary. The Kurds are, of course, organizing, and they are defending themselves. But the international public is shut out and sometimes does not see what is happening over there. There is a serious attempt on the part of the traditional colonizers of Kurdistan to eliminate the Kurds, and it gets scary, because the hegemonic powers, including the United States of America, also don't want the Kurdish project to get any traction. I liken the situation to just before World War I, when the Soviet Union arose out of the instability of the world system.

Democratic confederalism in that sense is a social and political system that does not just involve the Kurds. It's not based on ethnicity. As I said, it's based on three principles: democracy, women's freedom, and ecology. There are grassroots, horizontal, and vertical organizations and institutions to ensure that society becomes functional again. It has been suppressed for so long that the only way left to be political is parliamentary elections. Just go and cast your vote. But they want to make politics functional again, to reinvigorate politics, along with the morality of society. They want to set the pace of social lawmaking, to take that back into their hands, not to do it as suits various interest groups within a given state.

Sasha: *You said earlier that, for better or for worse, the Kurds didn't have the backing of a great power, and that so much of the* *politics of ethnicity and nationhood and who got nationhood in the twentieth century has, of course, been complicated by the fact that you have these great powers operating behind the scenes. The US created a complication in the Syrian conflict by giving material support to the Kurds who were fighting against ISIS, which raises the question of whether that in any way compromises the Kurdish freedom movement. I would like to ask you that question. I would also like to ask you if there is a danger that with its complex calculation about backing different forces, often both sides against each other, the US might back the Kurds to leverage its power through them and do the same thing with other entities at the same time?*

Havin: Yes, it may look paradoxical, but when you look at what is really happening there, Syria will not be the decisive battleground anyway. Plus, nobody is really fighting in Syria just for Syria; they are doing it for themselves—especially Iran and Turkey and, thus, Russia and the United States as well. In the midst of this whole power game, the Kurds are finding themselves grappling for their lives. They have made the same choice as they did in Lebanon, in the Beqaa Valley, to stand with the project of plurality, coexistence, and so on. They have actually talked to all the powers involved a number of times, not just the United States of America. They have no problem talking to anybody.

From 2013 to 2015, Abdullah Öcalan and the PKK had very serious talks with Turkey about negotiations to resolve the Kurdish question. They talked to Iran. They talked to Iraq. They are still talking to Syria. They talk to Russia, and just as there is a representative of the Kurds in Northern Syria here in the US, there is also one in Russia. They are talking to everybody. Of course, this warfare is created by these powers. It's their guns that are being used to attack the Kurds, and it is their guns that the fighters are buying to defend themselves. It's their guns they are getting to fight against their guns. People see this. It's not that people don't see this, but I think that what you also have to look at is whether there is any compromise in the project. At this point, the actual battleground is over Rojava. Everybody is trying to appropriate and co-opt the revolution. You find yourself deep in these waters, and you can't say, "I'm not going to play the game." However, the game is only played to the degree that it means life or death. Of course, this is always the case. It's either that or allowing Turkey to come into Afrin to weaken the revolution. What was Afrin and Turkey all about? It wasn't just about Russia; it was also about the US. They are trying to make sure that this revolution does not survive, so it constantly needs to protect itself from attacks from outside. About these paradoxical issues, though, we ourselves need to step in, as do the different democratic and left-wing forces and movements, and not to say, "If the Kurds are talking to them, we are just going to abandon the Kurds" or whatever. Because the situation there is a battle for life in every sense.

Postscript, January 2021

Sasha: *Much has happened since I spoke with you two years ago. In October of 2019, after the United States withdrew its tactical backing of the Kurds, Turkish forces invaded and occupied part of Rojava. How serious a setback has that been?*

Havin: World War III in the Middle East has culminated on many fronts and many levels. First among them are the contradictions and relations related to the US, the chaos empire, and the other global powers that have set their eyes on hegemony, both in the region and, as a result, around the world. Similar contradictions and relations exist among the regional powers in the Middle East, particularly in the case of Turkey, which would like to take advantage of the situation to become a regional empire. Another factor is the fundamental contradiction between the US-led chaos empire, which would like to change the status quo in the region, as the regimes in the region that are resisting no longer benefit the world order and the pro-status quo regimes. However, this is not a progressive resistance, as some might like to believe. These regimes, which gained and maintained power as a result of the bipolar balance of power after the two world wars, have brought nothing but impoverishment to most of society, the women and the youth, as well as to the various ethnic groups, including the Kurds. Of course, the other important factor in this equation is the desire of people, the women, the youth, the workers, the peasants, and everyone else to rid themselves of these exploitative, colonial, and imperial forces and to establish their own way of life, led by the Kurdish freedom movement in the region. The struggle, contradictions, and relations among all these different forces will determine what kind of a system emerges from the chaos in the Middle East and will certainly have an overall influence on the world system.

Therefore, we should primarily see this as a transitional phase, with everything that is happening constituting a transition from the old status quo to a new one. We are not there yet. The chaos and the crisis are continuing and spiraling. One of the forces that is responsible for this chaos and much of the bloodshed is the Turkish state and its respective governments. Of course, we also witnessed how the Arab Spring in 2011 was turned against the people by the nation-state pro-status quo regimes in the region in the form of the destruction of their lives, forced migration and the creation of refugees, or death at home or when fleeing abroad. In this context, the role the Turkish state played from Middle East to Africa garnered the support of the Western capitalist powers under the leadership of the US and Russia—the other capitalist power. The fascist forces with Islamic roots (al-Nusra, the Syria National Army, al-Qaeda, ISIS, etc.) also received consistent support from any number of these powers and turned into proxies used to attain concessions from one another. The forces involved in a struggle to redesign the Middle East in their interests coalesced as a joint force against women, peoples, workers, peasants, the true democracy forces who have been exploited, colonized, oppressed, and deemed nonexistent. They are in the ugliest, dirtiest, and most brutal of partnerships against the possibility of a new October revolution in the Middle East. The anti-Kurdish and antidemocratic policies implemented in Northern Kurdistan by the Turkish state have now boiled over into the autonomous regions in northeastern Syria, part of the Syrian nation-state, and also increasingly into Southern Kurdistan into the Iraqi federal state.

The main danger until the first few months of 2019 was the ISIS attacks and its occupation of Rojava and throughout the north and east of Syria. The Turkish state implemented and continues to implement its anti-Kurdish and anti-democratic policies through ISIS and its support and protection of fascists with Islamic roots. Turkey is the patron of these fascist gangs. It uses these gangs to invade and occupy the living areas of both the Kurds and the Arabs in the region; for example, the Kurdish cities of Afrin and Serekani and the Arab cities of Jarabulus and al-Bab have all been occupied. These invasions and occupations have been the achievement of the proven partnership of Turkey with ISIS. However, we shouldn't think that this is an independent initiative that does not have the approval of Russia and the US, both of which have been extremely silent. With this silence and the arms deals they have indicated their approval of these developments.

At the beginning of 2019, a new period began in Syria when the Syrian Democratic Forces (SDF) and the international coalition forces freed Raqqa, and then, with the Dera Zor-Baxoz operations, defeated ISIS and ended its rule. This was important, because it was meant to set in motion a new political solution in Syria. The joint struggle of the SDF and the US-led international coalition was militarily focused on the fight against ISIS. However, this military cooperation did not lead to cooperation toward finding a political solution. On the contrary, the coalition did not recognize the democratic will of the Kurdish people or of the other peoples in Syria. Thus, there is a divergence around finding a political solution to the situation in Syria. The SDF and the political forces in Rojava and northeast Syria have been clear about their intentions from the beginning.

In the new period, following the defeat of ISIS, there is a political-ideological contradiction and disagreement between the policies of the capitalist powers in designing Syria and the Middle East and the system of democratic autonomy being built in Rojava and the whole of northeast Syria. The autonomous system in Rojava based on democratic confederalism is an alternative system for women, peoples, belief systems, and all of the other sections of the society and a road map for women, laborers, and oppressed people that is taking concrete form in Rojava in the twenty-first century. That is why the US- and Russian-led capitalist powers and the local nation-states under Turkish leadership (including Syria, Iran, and more recently Iraq, to a certain degree) have joined their efforts and are working together to bring this system down and eliminate it. Turkey—the chief guardian of the nation-state model—has been chosen as the frontline force for intervention and occupation in these regions. Because Turkey is a NATO member, the US hopes to use it as an obstacle to Russia's influence, and so, in an effort to benefit from all of this, remains silent about Turkey's state terror and its war crimes and dirty dealing. Of course, the US also offers its support to better control Turkey in the service of its own plans to redesign the Middle East.

In 2018, the city of Afrin was occupied by the Turkish army and the Al-Nusra (or what is now called Tahrir al-Sham), followed by the occupation of the Gri Spi and Serekaniye city centers, on October 9, 2019. Civilians were killed during the invasion and occupation, and thousands of Kurdish, Assyrian, Turkmen, and Arab people who did not support these forces were displaced. These occupations were supported by powers who at the outset seemed to oppose one another. Today, the whole international machinery is looking the other way as Afrin is pillaged. Turkey treats the Kurdish homeland as booty, pillaging its olives and selling the women, just as ISIS sold the Yazidi women. Russia, for example, hopes to use the attacks of the Turkish army and its gangs to put pressure on the autonomous administration in northeast Syria, so that everything can return to the previous status quo. They are literally saying, "Hand the administration of the cities back to Damascus, and retreat from your demands for a democratic solution." Meanwhile, the US, for its part, is trying to prevent Turkey from drifting closer to Russia and continues to use Turkey as the front line in its designs for the Middle East. Furthermore, everyone is benefiting from the pillaging, whatever form it takes. Therefore, Turkey seems to want to conclude the genocide of the peoples it has begun and to totally eliminate the Assyrians and the Armenians from its territory, but, even more so, to eradicate the Kurds, because their sheer numbers and the spread of their homeland constitutes a threat, in and of itself. So the genocide of the Kurds and denying them any social or political status is supported by these powers for a variety of reasons.

There can be no doubt that the invasion of Gri Spi and Serekaniye, on October 9, 2019, led to serious losses for the autonomous administration. The plan to detach different parts of Rojava from one another is moving forward. After Afrin, an attempt was made to detach the cantons of Kobanî and Cizire. This is part of what the Turkish state calls the "collapsing plan," and it has not been implemented in Rojava alone; it was also implemented in the north after the talks with Öcalan and the PKK collapsed. It is said to be based on the model the Sri Lankan state used against the Tamil people. It also exists in particular ways in the south and in the north of Iraq. People in the region saw yet again that the approach of the powers, such as the US and Russia, was not intended to achieve peace and democracy and totally disregards their will for a democratic solution. The only peaceful and democratically developing areas in the region are being targeted and pulled into war and backwardness. This has, of course, created a huge amount of anger and proved to those affected just how right they were to not depend on anyone but themselves.

The situation in Southern Kurdistan and northern Iraq is also worth mentioning. The traditional Kurdish power holders in Southern Kurdistan have also sided with the Turkish state. This may sound strange, but if we look at it from a ruler's point of view rather than an ethnic point of view it makes perfect sense. As I have said many times, people no longer want to be ruled in this manner. Although the gains in Southern Kurdistan were very important for Kurdish people's aspirations, and the attempts to make Iraq a federation could be more democratized, this was a chance wasted by the elitist Kurdish rulers in Southern Kurdistan. Instead of developing democracy and addressing the needs of the people, their ongoing policy was one of repressing society and ensuring that it remains dysfunctional, while embracing relationships that will consolidate their power and corruption. Thus, we are seeing the Partiya Demokrat a Kurdistanê (Democratic Party of Kurdistan; KDP) and the Barzani family, as well as the YNK, entering into all sorts of relationships that undermine the aspirations of not only the region but of the Kurdish people themselves. They are now negotiating with the Iraqi state to destroy the autonomous character of the Shengal areas. Turkey is trying to hasten this, both with the KDP and the Iraqi federal government. Indeed, by using the KDP in all of this—and the advantage for KDP is that they get to stay in power longer as a puppet regime—Turkey is also taking advantage of well-worn divide and conquer politics. Turkey now has over fifty military bases in Southern Kurdistan and northern Iraq. The KDP has invited the US to station its military forces on the border with Rojava, and the people in Southern Kurdistan have shown their discomfort recently with huge protests because of the grievances they experience in Southern Kurdistan.

The revolutionary and counterrevolutionary struggles continue in Rojava. In this sense, and in the light of what we have been discussing throughout this book, this situation is far from permanent; as yet, it is not at the point where we can speak of an ultimate or a final gain or a loss, so there is a period of ongoing struggle ahead. There have been important losses on all sides, as well as some steps forward or backward throughout the region.

At the same time, of course, internally, the revolution in Rojava, in northeast Syria, continues on the basis of huge resistance. Despite all the threats, first and foremost to their lives, by a number of forces, including Damascus, the people there are adamant about staying on the lands they have lived on forever. The rebuilding in the autonomous areas continues on every front—political, social, economic, educational, health, self-defense—but, of course, the danger lingers. The people are aware that, on the one hand, there is the threat of genocide and of being driven out of their homelands and, on the other hand, of the need to defend their existence there, to drive the colonizers out of all the occupied areas, and to free themselves—the continuous source of their struggle. What we are witnessing is that even under occupation and extreme hardship resistance against the occupiers continues.

The attacks by the Turkish state and its thugs against democratic confederalism, on the one hand, and the attempt to construct a democratic nation, on the other hand, continue. Presently, this can be seen in the form of attacks against Ayn Issa. There are military attacks against this city at this very moment. At the same time, there is also far-reaching self-defense going on. It looks like the entire Middle East will be increasingly turned into a battlefield, as the people do not and will not accept regimes that are worse than the ones they have

Therefore, we should not so much ⟨…⟩ ⟨…⟩ned liberated areas but, rather, a strug- ⟨…⟩nary and counterrevolutionary forces. It ⟨…⟩ will witness major struggles, and the battle is far fr⟨…⟩ver. I guess that if humans continue to exist there will always be yearning to be free, and this means there will be ongoing struggle.

Sasha: *You argue that the strength of the Kurdish movement lies in not being beholden to any nation-state. But hasn't the experiment in Rojava been dependent, by default, on the Syrian government?*

Havin: The goal of the revolution and the experiment in Rojava is not to establish a new nation-state, nor is it to destroy the Syrian nation-state. The goal is to transform the Syrian regime, so that it favors a new system based on democracy, freedom, and equality. It is, of course, important that we understand the history of the Middle East, and that there will not be a quick and easy solution. We must go through a period of struggle that transforms traditional mentalities and overcomes traditional forces in the region and the established approach of the global powers to the region's people and rulers.

In general, the Kurdish freedom movement believes that there is a relationship among all living beings in the universe; they influence one another, and so there is a relationship encompassing all things. Therefore, absolute independence is not something that is possible for anything. This is also true in terms of social history. The Kurdish movement for democracy and freedom is not focused on establishing a separate state in any part of Kurdistan, but it does target the creation of an area where the peoples, women, and all sections of society are able to think and talk about themselves and their needs in terms of democracy and freedom and act on their conclusions. Thus, the freedom movement struggles for society's right to govern itself without a state. It puts forth the formula of state *plus* democracy as, in fact, constituting two different things. They are saying that the state is not needed to have a functioning democracy, and achieving this objective would allow them to reanimate society without sliding back into a state. Strengthenening the functionality of democracy and society, what the freedom movement calls moral and political society's self-governance is so vital, so that there is equilibrium between the state and democracy. At the moment, the society and, thus, democracy are nonexistent, and the state has expanded to encompass all areas. Obviously, the people in the area are not expecting the various global and regional powers to change overnight and agree to this, but there is a huge struggle to at least make these states receptive to democracy, so that they don't become unwavering obstacles.

This is why the freedom movement that is waging the struggle in the Middle East is adamant about not being dependent on any one power. Its objective is to wage a far-reaching struggle both to transform society and to further the struggle for democracy and the transformation of the region, at times, cooperatively, and at other times, in contradiction, including the possibility of war with various powers—although, understandably, we would like to avoid this, if at all possible. This is the only option; there is no easy way to achieve this. It is the culmination of thousands of years of struggles in the Middle East, and there is a dire need need of a Renaissance for the Middle East. This could also be viewed the Renaissance of the Middle East, as life can no longer go on in the region as it has been. This is why relationships with nation-states are not completely out of the question in politics or economics or any other area of life. The situation in Rojava is not about two states, but is a question of an autonomous region within a state, with the goal of transforming the Syrian state. The Rojava model is, of course, a model of a system of living, production, and sharing in which power relations don't develop. Whenever nation-states do not accept this and, instead, enforce their rule without heeding organized society's needs and requirements, there is and will be self-defense. Thus, instead of dependence, they are trying to build a voluntary union, living together side by side, acknowledging one another's will and reestablishing relationship on that basis.

So, no, the model is not dependent on the Syrian government, but it is important to maintain a relationship that makes the extension of democracy to all of Syria more likely than a direct military conflict with the nation-state.

Sasha: *How would you assess the successes and failures of the Rojava revolution at this point? What has been most enduring?*
Havin: As we can see, the Rojava revolution is far from complete but is a continuing and continuous one. In the aftermath of the collapse of real socialism, there was a huge ideological propaganda attack of the capitalist system with the claim that the Age of Ideology was over, and that socialism and any idea of revolution were played out. The Rojava revolution was, in this sense, very important to the whole world; it showed everyone that revolution was still possible, even in the least expected of places. Of course, it was not really the least expected place, because there has been a huge struggle there for almost half a century now. A long while ago, Öcalan said that twenty-first century would be the century of women and peoples, which the Rojava revolution, in fact, verifies, setting in motion the process by which this prediction will come true. Revolutions, socialism, communalism, people's desire for a free life are not lost. The Rojava revolution shows us the contrary. Starting with Kurdistan and the Middle East, it gave people throughout the world the hope that it is, in fact, possible to build one's own modernity. It also showed that revolutions neither needed to take over state power nor to destroy or conquer it but could build something outside of it, and, in this way, created new space and laid the groundwork for a new October Revolution. We could perhaps say that this is the primary victory of the

Rojava revolution; that it clearly and powerfully established a third way—making the ideological, political, self-defense, and social aspects concrete. It showed that if there is to be a revolution it has to be led by a women's revolution—especially in the Middle East. It is a fact that without a woman's revolution no revolution can have a strong basis. This needs to continue all the more strongly, even and especially after the initial stages of the revolution. To overcome sexism and its institutionalization, the struggle needs to continue and must become an aspect of social change and be institutionalized in a revolutionary manner.

As such, it is important that differences and diversities are recognized by distinct systems and lifestyles but intertwined with a common life system. There is a beautiful stream in Kurdistan called the Avaşin; two streams flow together to become the Avaşin, but neither loses its color, and they flow side by side.

The Rojava revolution has shown us that people can live side by side, that they are receptive to woman's freedom, that their approach to religion need not be based on rejection and denial, and that they can live side by side as distinct groups like the waters of the Avaşin. This new understanding of nationhood, which Öcalan calls the democratic nation, becoming concrete was also very important. The approach to self-defense and the clarification of an understanding of violence was another very important issue, as was the fact that one should neither rely on states nor make the revolution and then expect others to do the work but, rather, engage and struggle as part of a society, with all of its constituents intact, to free life and oneself in the process.

As I said earlier, this is far from over; the structural crisis of capitalism has culminated in huge chaos, which gives the oppressed and colonized a window of opportunity, as a result of their struggles over the century. The outcome of this chaos will be determined by these struggles, and the establishment of a new equilibrium around the world and in the region. So there is still a lot to do, especially in terms of the development of the internal dynamics; there is a huge attack in the region that threatens the very lives of the people and society as a whole, which does not easily allow for the necessary social transformation and change. Therefore, social transformation is not yet sufficient and must continue. Establishing an ecological way of life seems impossible under the threat of ethnic cleansing and with the use of all kinds of weapons, but there is now an understanding that the options are an ecological way of life or the total fascism of Turkish state and its proxies, including ISIS. The very real threat of genocide blocks a Renaissance in the region. The states, first and foremost the Turkish state, the most backward force in the region, are completely resistant to the development of democracy.

Sasha: *What is the future of the liberation struggle in Rojava and beyond?*
Havin: This is a question that we must be answer together with all the other forces that are waging a freedom struggle. What will all these forces do in the face of a World War III? Will they wait for their turn or work together to strengthen the revolution? The colonialism, male domination, imperialism, racism, and fascism that are determining all of our futures are becoming global in their actions. These powers are acting in unison to suppress the reawakened aspirations of women, youth, and peoples, so those who are struggling must also find ways to act in unison.

Is it a matter of solely watching what is happening to the Kurds in the Middle East and to clap when they are successful, and when there is a setback to become disillusioned? This whole situation is beyond that.

Ways to act together must be found, to complete and complement one another, and to develop a way of thinking, feeling, and doing on a universal scale. It is essential that this succeeds, as it will determine our shared future. There is nothing prepre-pared or predetermined. There is no guarantee of absolute victory or absolute defeat. The only guarantee will come from the struggles that are waged and how they communicate with one another. These struggles and this resistance will deter-mine our collective future.

One thing is certain, we should continue to think well, talk well, do the best we can and never deviate from that. It may seem hopeless, but it is the nature of power and violence to make people feel that no matter what they do they cannot change anything, that the regime they face is eternal. As Öcalan often says, "What is victory? It is to raise your consciousness, to educate yourself, to attain ideological depth, to free your own thoughts and mind, to be able to organize yourself and those around you, and to actually have the courage to believe in victory and to insistently wage a struggle to that end."

It is already clear that 2021 will indeed be a difficult year, and there will be attacks on numerous levels. At present, it seems that the US, Russia, and Turkey have agreed on the anni-hilation of the Kurdish people's revolution, including in Rojava. They began working toward this in 2020, however, their plan failed to gain traction. Even when the collaborationist Kurdish forces in Southern Kurdistan were more clearly integrated into the plan agreed upon by Trump's US and Erdoğan's Turkey toward the end of the year, it did not take root. They could not divert the Rojava revolution from revolutionary democratic confederalism. There were also heavy attacks against the PKK guerrilla forces, but, in spite of losses, the PKK was not elimi-nated nor did it capitulate.

The people's choice is clear though. At a certain point, Erdoğan and his party had huge support, because he prom-ised to address the numerous questions that were waiting for a solution. Today, just like all the other governments in Turkey, Erdoğan and his AKP have totally lost support and must rely on violence and repression to rule Turkey and expand in the Middle East and Africa. He has nothing to offer the people except pain and suffering and the exploitation of their resources. As with Trump, this cannot and will not last. In spite of their extensive use of the available state mechanisms to polarize society and institutionalize themselves, this is proving ineffective. Therefore, 2021 will witness the intensification of these contradictions and struggles that will determine how we come out of this age of unreason that calls itself otherwise. Continuing to build our own system will be intertwined with self-defense. There is no alternative, is there? Neither surrender nor hopelessness are an option.

Political Biography of Abdullah Öcalan

Abdullah Öcalan was born on April 4, 1948, in the village of Amara, in the Xelfetî district of Riha (Urfa). He graduated from Ankara Anatolian Land Registry and Cadastre Vocational High School in 1968. In 1970, while working as a civil servant, he enrolled in the Faculty of Law at Istanbul University. During these years, he met with the Devrimci Doğu Kültür Ocağı (Revolutionary Cultural Eastern Hearths; DDKO) and the youth leaders of the 1968 generation about the Kurdish question.

He later quit the Faculty of Law and enrolled in the Faculty of Political Science at Ankara University. There he led a student strike protesting the March 1972 massacre of the Turkish revolutionary leader Mahir Çayan—whose ideas greatly influenced Öcalan and whom he commemorates to this day—and nine of his comrades in Kızıldere. On April 7, 1972, Abdullah Öcalan was imprisoned for seven months for his role in the protests.

Following his release from prison, having failed to introduce the Kurdish problem onto the agenda of Turkish revolutionaries, he started working on establishing a separate group around the idea that "Kurdistan is a colony." The historically important first meeting of this group took place in 1973, in Ankara. Kemal Pir's assertion that "the liberation of the Turkish people depends upon the liberation of the Kurdish people" provided the group's theoretical framework, and, in

1975, Abdullah Öcalan and Mehmet Hayri Durmuş penned the group's first written document titled "Analyses of Imperialism and Colonialism."[1]

In 1977, Öcalan and his friends traveled to Kurdistan to engage a campaign to raise awareness of the newly forming group and its ideas. Speeches Öcalan gave during this Kurdistan campaign were transcribed. He visited Bazîd (Elazığ), Qers (Kars), Dugor (Digor), Dersim, Çewlîg (Bingöl), Xarpêt (Harput), Amed (Diyarbakır), Mêrdin (Mardin), Riha (Urfa), and Dîlok (Antep). Abdullah Öcalan's "The Way of the Kurdistan Revolution," also known as the "Manifesto," was written in the summer of 1978 and published in the first issue of the journal *Serxwebûn* (Independence).

Abdullah Öcalan wrote the "Party Program" in memory of Haki Karer, who was from the Black Sea Region and had been murdered in Dîlok, and declared the foundation of Partîya Karkerên Kurdîstan (Kurdistan Workers' Party; PKK) at a congress in the village of Fis, in Amed, on November 26–27, 1978. In the wake of the declaration, the Turkish state carried out massacres in Maraş and Meletî (Malatya) and attacks in Semsûr (Adıyaman) and Xarpêt, and then declared martial law and detained numerous people.[2] In 1979, foreseeing a military coup, which would indeed occur in 1980, Abdullah Öcalan and several of his friends passed through the border town Pirsus (Suruç) into the city of Kobanî, in Syria.

After leaving Turkey, from 1979 to 1998, Öcalan organized and led the political education of the PKK's rank and file, which he considered more important than military training. At the same time, he also led the movement as a whole, conducted foreign relations and was responsible for diplomatic meetings, while doing his best to stay in touch with Kurds and allies in Lebanon, Syria, and, increasingly, around the world.

Going back and forth between Syria and Lebanon, where he cooperated with the Palestinian Liberation Organization and met with new and old cadres for the coming struggle,

Abdullah Öcalan began making the preparations for a revolutionary people's war against junta set up after the September 12, 1980, coup d'état. During the same period, he published the brochure *United Front of Resistance against Fascism*. In 1981, he wrote the books *The Role of Force in Kurdistan, The Question of Personality in Kurdistan, Life in the Party and the Characteristics of the Revolutionary Militant*, and *The Problem of National Liberation and the Road Map to its Resolution*, as well as his political report to the party's first conference. In the following two years, he also penned the works *On Organization* (1982) and *On Gallows and the Culture of the Barracks* (1983).

The military coup resulted in thousands of people being imprisoned and severely tortured, as a wave of severe repression was unleashed against society. News of disappearances and executions were leaked despite intense censorship. As a result, Öcalan's writings in this period focused on how to build an armed organization against fascism, how to fight against the Kurdish landowners and aristocracy who collaborated with the state, and how to transform the Kurdish militants, with their oppressed and colonized personalities, into freedom fighters. He also made several attempts to build a coalition with the Turkish revolutionary organizations that had succeeded in crossing into other countries in the region. However, internal disputes in the Turkish left, among other things, prevented the emergence of such a coalition. Then, on August 15, 1984, the PKK carried out its first armed offensive against two military posts, one in Dih (Eruh) and the other in Şemzînan (Şemdinli). Thereafter, the PKK began to grow exponentially.

As the organization continued to grow steadily from 1987 to 1990, gaining popularity among Kurds and extending its regional influence, new problems emerged. A series of documents with the title "Analyses" assembled Öcalan's intense discussion of the existing problems. These documents were later published as brochures, including *The Revolutionary Approach to Religion* and *The Question of Woman and the*

Family, and as books titled *The Liquidation of Liquidationism, The Fascism of September 12 and the PKK's Resistance, Betrayal and Collaboration in Kurdistan*, and *Selected Writings*, vols. 1–4.

The PKK's armed struggle against the Turkish state continued even after the military coup was nominally ended. In terms of the repression that Kurds faced in the region, the banning of their language and their organizations and the denial of their existence, the transition to democracy in 1984 was a nonevent. Indeed, not only the PKK but the entire left in Turkey defined the post–military coup period as the institutionalization of fascism and neoliberalism in Turkey. From 1990 to 1992, the armed struggle Öcalan led, which he called "a war for the protection of existence," gained massive popular support. During this period, Öcalan became convinced that the political solutions to the Kurdish question that the PKK proposed and the strategies it had adopted needed to be revised. This phase saw Öcalan's *Resurrection Is Complete, Now It's Time for Liberation* and the 1993 book-length interview with Yalçın Küçük titled *The Story of the Resurrection*. In these books, Öcalan started to conceptualize a radical form of democracy that could liberate Kurds, women, and other oppressed groups.

In the early 1990s, Öcalan gave several interviews to Turkish journalists and leftists regarding his search for a democratic solution and efforts to achieve peace, which were published as the following books: *Meetings with Abdullah Öcalan* (Doğu Perinçek, 1990); *Apo and the PKK* (Mehmet Ali Birand, 1992); *Interview in a Kurdish Garden* (Yalçın Küçük, 1993); *The Kurdish Question with Öcalan and Burkay* (Oral Çalışlar, 1993); *I am Looking for a Collocutor: Ceasefire Talks* (1994); *Killing the Man* (Mahir Sayın, 1997). During those years, his analysis of communality also left its mark on the Kurdish community, and he published *Problems of Revolution and Socialism, Insisting on Socialism Is Insisting on Being Human, The Language and Action of Revolution, History Is Hidden in Our Day and We are Hidden at History's Beginning, How to Live*, vols. 1 and 2, and *Kurdish Love*.[3]

As can be deduced from the titles of the books, at this point, Öcalan was primarily concentrating on two aspects of the struggle: first, how to center on women's freedom and transform the PKK into an organization that can provide freedom to its militants and to the people; second, how to deal with the shortcomings of the Soviet real socialist model without giving up the ideals of a socialist revolution. He also started developing his ideas about history, which he would later return to in much greater detail in his prison writings.

Öcalan states that the second half of 1990s was when he obtained his own freedom, in the sense of freeing himself from dogmatic thinking. During this period, he tried to open up a venue for dialogue between the PKK and the Turkish state. The book *Dialogues, Ceasefire Statements, and Press Releases, 1993, 1995, and 1998* is a compilation of Öcalan's analyses in the context of the attempts made at dialogue with the governments of President Turgut Özal (1993) and Prime Ministers Necmettin Erbakan (1995) and Bülent Ecevit (1998). All of these efforts were sabotaged by events that the Kurdish Movement and Öcalan have a strong suspicion were the work of NATO/Gladio units.[4] Major examples of such events are the massacre of thirty-three unarmed Turkish soldiers by a PKK guerrilla group, the suspicious death of Özal, and the attacks, bombings, and assassination attempts targeting Abdullah Öcalan. The attacks against Öcalan and his ideas by forces that aimed to prevent peace and democracy in Kurdistan culminated in Öcalan's exile from the Middle East and his eventual abduction. The US's multidimensional diplomatic and military pressure on the Syrian state, including Turkey's open threat of war against Damascus, meant Abdullah Öcalan had to leave Syria on October 9, 1998.

Abduction and Detention

After leaving Syria, Öcalan looked for a new place where he could continue the political struggle. The details of the international diplomacy he conducted for a democratic solution to the Kurdish question and peace in Turkey during this period are published as a book titled *Towards Peace: The Rome Talks*. During this period, the CIA and Mossad pursued him relentlessly, and, as a result of the intense pressure applied by NATO and Turkey, different governments forced him to leave. After an odyssey through several European countries, Öcalan set off for South Africa, but he was never to arrive. On February 15, 1999, in a plot that involved several secret services, including the CIA, Mossad, and Turkish and Greek intelligence agencies, he was abducted while leaving the Greek embassy in Kenya, Nairobi, and handed over to Turkey. The abduction caused protests and uprisings by Kurds in all four parts of Kurdistan and worldwide.

A Trial and the Death Penalty

On June 29, 1999, Abdullah Öcalan was sentenced to death after a short show trial on İmralı Island in Turkey. The trial was later ruled as not fair and impartial by the Grand Chamber of the European Court of Human Rights (ECtHR). Meanwhile, Kurdish protest reached its peak, and Turkey declared that as part of the negotiations for its ascension to member state status in the EU, it was considering abolishing the death penalty. Indeed, in 2002, the death penalty was abolished, and, as a result, the judiciary commuted Öcalan's sentence to "aggravated life imprisonment," without any possibility of early release—in other words: imprisonment until death. The ECtHR condemned this inhumane punishment in 2013, but its ruling has not had any tangible consequence as of yet.

Prison Conditions on the Prison Island of İmralı

Abdullah Öcalan's prison conditions are grim, and he is confronted with an arbitrary regime of total isolation. İmralı Island, where he is imprisoned, is a restricted military zone located in the Sea of Marmara. Öcalan spent the first ten years of his sentence as the only prisoner on the island, guarded by more than one thousand soldiers. In 2009, a new prison was built for him, and there are now three other prisoners on the island. All cells in this new prison are designed for solitary confinement. Each of the prisoners has his own tiny courtyard for fresh air, but due to the extreme height of the walls these yards look like well shafts.

Öcalan still cannot receive letters and is the only prisoner in Turkey without access to a telephone. In the last ten years, the authorities have only permitted five meetings with his lawyers and five family visits, and these were only made possible by the protracted hunger strikes of several thousand Kurdish political prisoners spread across Turkey.

Despite these conditions, Öcalan has produced a major corpus of writings while in prison.[5] Starting with his defense speech in the show trial on İmralı Island, *The Declaration on the Democratic Solution of the Kurdish Question* (1999), these writings outline the new strategy that the PKK and other actors in the Kurdish freedom movement should adopt to transform Kurdistan, Turkey, and the broader region without changing existing political borders. *Prison Writings: The Roots of Civilization* is an extensive historical and philosophical study that lays the groundwork for all of the following books, while its second volume, *The PKK and the Kurdish Question in the 21st Century* (both 2001), extensively evaluated and critiqued the PKK's shortcomings and failures, in order to improve its social impact and increase its political capacity. His submission to the Greek courts, *Defense of the Free Human* (2003), shed more light on his abduction and the role of various powers and further developed the ideas he had previously addressed. Öcalan's subsequent writings further delved into and developed his thesis about history and began to map out his alternative paradigm, first in *Beyond State, Power, and Violence* (2004).[6] This book played a major role in forming what he calls a "new kind of revolutionary party." Bringing together ideas from prominent

Western and non-Western scholars, he argued for an under-standing of history as an antagonism between state formation and society formation. Since revolution is for the empower-ment of society, it also should be against the state, organizing in a way that renders the state redundant. While capitalism, patriarchy, and the nation-state build capitalist modernity, he argues that the people's resistance against these systems should build upon the history of democratic modernity, of which the world's revolutionary struggles are the heir. Finally, in his writings, Öcalan also revisited and further developed his ideas on women's freedom and revolution—which he called his "unfinished project." Putting women's freedom and revolution at the center of all democratic revolutions, he emphasized that women's autonomous organization and ideological produc-tion will transform society into a state of equality, peace, and freedom. All these ideas are mapped out in the five-volume *Manifesto of the Democratic Civilization* (2008–2011).[7]

The ideas that Öcalan formulated in prison have greatly influenced and inspired three revolutionary projects. The Northeast Syria project, more commonly known as the Rojava revolution, under the leadership of Kurds, with the participa-tion of different peoples, including Arabs and Assyrians, is a revolution where the role of women and the youth continues to determine the direction, and which serves as beacon of hope for the region. The Halkların Demokratik Partisi (Peoples' Democratic Party; HDP), which was founded in 2012 and brings the Kurdish movement together with other freedom move-ments in Turkey, including socialist, women's, ecological, and LGBTQI+ movements, Alevis, Armenians, and other opposi-tion movements led by the peoples themselves, and which has received the support of 12 percent of the electorate in Turkey, is also shaped by Öcalan's ideas. Another example, the Kurdish Yazidi people's autonomous council, formed in the aftermath of attacks, is oriented toward self-defence and self-government, so that Yazidis can continue to flourish on their land. For its part, the Kurdish women's movement, equipped with Öcalan's analysis, not only set a precedent in self-organization and self-defence under the current conditions but also showed how to translate this into political mechanisms that allow women to exert their weight for a lasting transformation in the Middle East. All of these political actors aim to build democratic autonomous regions in the Middle East where radical democracy is exercised and to unite in a confederal structure on the basis of an ecological, feminist, and decolonial constitution.

Struggle for Peace

While in prison, Öcalan further developed and augmented the strategy that the Kurdish movement adopted during the second half of 1990s to achieve peace with the Turkish state. In 2009, he announced that he intended to write a document outlining a "road map" to peace and encouraged people to share their thoughts on the subject with him. This triggered an extensive debate in Turkey and abroad, which energized different sections of society. He completed the "road map" on August 15, 2009, the twenty-fifth anniversary of the launching of the armed struggle. This road map served as a basis for a process of dialogue with the state.

From 2009 to mid-2011, a delegation appointed by the Turkish government engaged in secret negotiations with Abdullah Öcalan on İmralı Island and with leading PKK members in Oslo (the so-called "Oslo process"). The parties involved agreed on several protocols. These protocols contained a step-by-step plan to end the armed conflict and make the necessary institutional transformation to resolve the Kurdish question. However, the Turkish government decided not to implement this plan, instead extending the waves of arrests of Kurdish politicians and activists and starting massive military operations in June 2011.

In another series of talks, Turkish state authorities conducted a direct dialogue with Öcalan on İmralı Island (the "İmralı process"). In late 2012, the state acknowledged that these talks had taken place. The assassination of three Kurdish female politicians, including PKK founding member Sakine Cansız, by the Turkish secret service, the MİT, in Paris on January 9, 2013, threatened to quickly bring the talks to a standstill, but Öcalan stuck with them.

At the Newroz festivities in March 2013, Öcalan called for the withdrawal of the armed groups from Turkey and expressed his hope for democratization in Turkey. The call was heeded, and hopes for peace resurfaced. That year, *Time* magazine named Öcalan as one of the one hundred most influential people in the world, and he was nominated for the Nobel Peace Prize.

In the following months, however, it became clear that the Turkish state's sole objective was to disarm the PKK, and that it had no interest in a political solution. The last pinnacle in the so-called "peace process" was the Dolmabahçe Declaration in February 2015, when an agreed protocol on peace was read in the presence of the vice prime minister, who was acting on the directive of then prime minister Recep Tayyip Erdoğan, and HDP lawmakers, who represented Öcalan.

However, soon afterward, then prime minister and later president of Turkey Recep Tayyip Erdoğan shifted strategy, scrapped the entire dialogue process, and renewed military escalation.

Protests and Campaigns

Since Abdullah Öcalan left Syria in 1998 and his subsequent arrest in 1999, there have been countless protests in Kurdistan, in Turkey, and internationally against his abduction, the death penalty, incommunicado detention on İmralı Island, targeted damage to his health, against total isolation, and in support of his political role and his freedom. On several occasions, the isolation could only be broken through protracted widespread hunger strike actions.

In a signature campaign conducted in 2005–2006, around 3.5 million people from all parts of Kurdistan signed a statement affirming that they regard Öcalan as their political representative. The number of signatures was remarkable considering that the campaign was conducted under immense restrictions—Turkey, Syria, and Iran declared it illegal. Several people were convicted and sentenced to seven years in prison in connection with the campaign.

In 2007, a hunger strike began in Strasbourg, France, to protest the ongoing poisoning of Öcalan, which had been substantiated by a laboratory.[8] A wave of protests quickly spread across Kurdistan, Turkey, and Europe. In a second hunger strike, which began in Strasbourg and Turkey, in 2012, more than seven hundred Kurdish prisoners and many ordinary Kurds all over the world demanded the right to speak their mother tongue and insisted that the Turkish state negotiate with Öcalan. Again, from late 2018 to early 2019, a hunger strike led by imprisoned HDP MP Leyla Güven and joined by thousands of people in prisons and outside of Turkey, demanded that isolation be lifted and Öcalan freed.

On June 25, 2012, Kurds began holding a daily vigil in front of the Council of Europe building in Strasbourg that continues until today. They are calling for Öcalan to be freed and are determined to continue the vigil until that goal is achieved.

On September 6, 2012, a signature campaign began, demanding "freedom for Abdullah Öcalan and the political prisoners in Turkey." The document states that "Öcalan's freedom will mark a breakthrough for the democratization of Turkey and peace in Kurdistan." More than 10.3 million people had signed by 2015.

Over the years, but especially since 2015, Abdullah Öcalan has received much recognition and a number of awards, including honorary citizenship in numerous Italian cities and towns, Palermo and Naples among them. On April 25, 2016, the GMB, a general trade union in the UK, with more than 622 thousand members, and Unite the Union, a British and Irish trade union with more than 1.2 million members, joined forces to launch the Freedom for Öcalan UK trade union campaign. The campaign was officially endorsed by the UK Trade Union Congress in September 2017, and more than fourteen of the largest trade unions in the UK have affiliated with the campaign.[9]

In early 2019, fifty Nobel laureates called for the end of the solitary confinement of Abdullah Öcalan and of all political prisoners in Turkey.

Meanwhile, leading intellectuals whose work Öcalan follows in spite of the challenges, including Immanuel Wallerstein, Barry K. Gills, Antonio Negri, John Holloway, and David Graeber, to name but a few, entered into a dialogue with Öcalan's ideas in the book *Building Free Life: Dialogues with Öcalan*, edited by the International Initiative "Freedom for Abdullah Öcalan—Peace in Kurdistan."[10] While he probably could not access the book, in the last visit that the lawyers were permitted with Öcalan, in 2019, he expressed his gratitude and declared his comradeship with all movements and people in the world who practice and fight for freedom.

As of today, Öcalan and the whole of İmralı Island remain in total isolation, with no possibility of communication whatsoever. Meanwhile, both support for his ideas and the chorus of voices calling for his freedom is growing every day.

Notes

1   Kemal Pir, a founding member of the PKK, in 1978, was a revolutionary from the Black Sea region of Turkey and ethnically a Laz. He lost his life on hunger strike in 1982 in the infamous Diyarbakır Military Prison. Mehmet Hayri Durmuş, a Kurdish revolutionary and member of the PKK also lost his life during this hunger strike.

2   The greatest massacre occurred in Maraş, where over one hundred members of the leftist oriented Alevi religious community were murdered by ultra-nationalists in a pogrom that lasted from December 19 to December 26, 1978.

3   In general, these books were informally published abroad and smuggled into Turkey and Kurdistan.

4   Operation Gladio is the codename for clandestine "stay-behind" operations that were organized by the Western Union (WU), and, subsequently, by NATO during the Cold War. All NATO member states built up units that were connected with anti-communist and far-right groups and politicians. In Turkey, these units became extremely influential as counter-guerrilla forces. The counter-guerrilla targets various leftist organizations, especially the PKK in Turkey and around Europe.

5   These books were written as submissions to various courts, mainly the European Court of Human Rights, where his case was being discussed.

6   PM Press published *Beyond State, Power, and Violence* in English in 2021.

7   *Civilization: The Age of Masked Gods and Disguised Kings*, vol. 1; *Capitalism: The Age of Unmasked Gods and Naked Kings*, vol. 2; *Sociology of Freedom*, vol. 3; *The Civilizational Crisis in the Middle East and the Democratic Civilization Solution*, vol. 4; *The Manifesto of the Kurdistan Revolution: Kurdish Question and the Solution of Democratic Nation*, vol. 5. All his books can be found at ocalanbooks. com.

8   Mahmut Şakar, "Press Statement by Öcalan's Lawyers: Öcalan Is Intoxicated," March 1, 2007, accessed December 15, 2020, http://www.freeocalan.org/articles/english/press-statement-by-ocalans-lawyers-ocalan-is-intoxicated; Pascal Kintz, "Statement of Dr. Pascal Kintz on Roj TV about His Analysis of the Ocalan Intoxication Results," March 1, 2007, accessed December 15, 2020, http://www.freeocalan.org/articles/english/analysis-of-ocalan-intoxication-results-by-dr-kintz.

9   For more details, see "Biography," International Initiative "Freedom for Abdullah Öcalan—Peace in Kurdistan," accessed February 7, 2021, https://freeocalan.org/biography.

10 International Initiative, ed., *Building Free Life: Dialogues with* Öcalan (Oakland: PM Press, 2020).

About the Contributors

Havin Guneser is an engineer, journalist, and women's rights activist who writes and speaks extensively about Abdullah Öcalan and the revolution in Rojava. She is one of the spokespersons for the International Initiative "Freedom for Abdullah Öcalan—Peace in Kurdistan" and the translator of several of Öcalan's books. She is on the advisory board of the journal *Jineoloji*.

Andrej Grubačič is professor and chair at the Anthropology and Social Change Department, California Institute of Integral Studies. He is the author of *Don't Mourn, Balkanize! Essays after Yugoslavia* (PM Press, 2010), the coauthor, with Staughton Lynd, of *Wobblies and Zapatistas: Conversations on Anarchism, Marxism and Radical History* (PM Press, 2008), and the coauthor, with Denis O'Hearn, of *Living at the Edges of Capitalism* (University of California Press, 2016).

Sasha Lilley is a writer and radio broadcaster. She's the cofounder and host of the critically acclaimed program of radical ideas *Against the Grain*. While program director of KPFA Radio, the flagship station of the Pacifica Network, she headed up award-winning national broadcasts, including "Winter Soldier: Iraq and Afghanistan." Sasha is the series editor of PM Press's political economy imprint, Spectre, and is the author of *Capital and Its Discontents* (PM Press, 2011), which *Publishers Weekly* called a "cool-headed but urgent volume—timely but sophisticated and wide-ranging enough to remain a longtime reference." She also coauthored the book *Catastrophism: The Apocalyptic Politics of Collapse and Rebirth* (PM Press, 2012).

ABOUT PM PRESS

PM Press is an independent, radical publisher of books and media to educate, entertain, and inspire. Founded in 2007 by a small group of people with decades of publishing, media, and organizing experience, PM Press amplifies the voices of radical authors, artists, and activists. Our aim is to deliver bold political ideas and vital stories to all walks of life and arm the dreamers to demand the impossible. We have sold millions of copies of our books, most often one at a time, face to face. We're old enough to know what we're doing and young enough to know what's at stake. Join us to create a better world.

PM Press
PO Box 23912
Oakland, CA 94623
www.pmpress.org

PM Press in Europe
europe@pmpress.org
www.pmpress.org.uk

FRIENDS OF PM PRESS

These are indisputably momentous times—the financial system is melting down globally and the Empire is stumbling. Now more than ever there is a vital need for radical ideas.

In the years since its founding—and on a mere shoestring—PM Press has risen to the formidable challenge of publishing and distributing knowledge and entertainment for the struggles ahead. With over 450 releases to date, we have published an impressive and stimulating array of literature, art, music, politics, and culture. Using every available medium, we've succeeded in connecting those hungry for ideas and information to those putting them into practice.

Friends of PM allows you to directly help impact, amplify, and revitalize the discourse and actions of radical writers, filmmakers, and artists. It provides us with a stable foundation from which we can build upon our early successes and provides a much-needed subsidy for the materials that can't necessarily pay their own way. You can help make that happen—and receive every new title automatically delivered to your door once a month—by joining as a Friend of PM Press. And, we'll throw in a free T-shirt when you sign up.

Here are your options:

- **$30 a month** Get all books and pamphlets plus 50% discount on all webstore purchases

- **$40 a month** Get all PM Press releases (including CDs and DVDs) plus 50% discount on all webstore purchases

- **$100 a month** Superstar—Everything plus PM merchandise, free downloads, and 50% discount on all webstore purchases

For those who can't afford $30 or more a month, we have **Sustainer Rates** at $15, $10 and $5. Sustainers get a free PM Press T-shirt and a 50% discount on all purchases from our website.

Your Visa or Mastercard will be billed once a month, until you tell us to stop. Or until our efforts succeed in bringing the revolution around. Or the financial meltdown of Capital makes plastic redundant. Whichever comes first.

DEPARTMENT OF ANTHROPOLOGY & SOCIAL CHANGE

Anthropology and Social Change, housed within the California Institute of Integral Studies, is a small innovative graduate department with a particular focus on activist scholarship, militant research, and social change. We offer both masters and doctoral degree programs.

Our unique approach to collaborative research methodology dissolves traditional barriers between research and political activism, between insiders and outsiders, and between researchers and protagonists. Activist research is a tool for "creating the conditions we describe." We engage in the process of co-research to explore existing alternatives and possibilities for social change.

Anthropology and Social Change
anth@ciis.edu
1453 Mission Street
94103
San Francisco, California
www.ciis.edu/academics/graduate-programs/anthropology-and-social-change

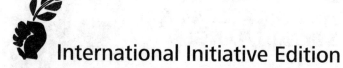

International Initiative Edition

International Initiative "Freedom for Abdullah Öcalan—Peace in Kurdistan" is a multinational peace initiative for the release of Abdullah Öcalan and a peaceful solution to the Kurdish question. It was established immediately after Öcalan was abducted in Kenya, Nairobi, and handed over to the Republic of Turkey on February 15, 1999, following a clandestine operation by an alliance of secret services. Part of its activity is the publication of Abdullah Öcalan's works.

The Sociology of Freedom: Manifesto of the Democratic Civilization, Volume III

Abdullah Öcalan
with a Foreword by John Holloway
Edited by International Initiative

ISBN: 978-1-62963-710-5
$28.95   480 pages

When scientific socialism, which for many years was implemented by Abdullah Öcalan and the Kurdistan Workers' Party (PKK), became too narrow for his purposes, Öcalan deftly answered the call for a radical redefinition of the social sciences. Writing from his solitary cell in İmralı Prison, Öcalan offered a new and astute analysis of what is happening to the Kurdish people, the Kurdish freedom movement, and future prospects for humanity.

The Sociology of Freedom is the fascinating third volume of a five-volume work titled *The Manifesto of the Democratic Civilization*. The general aim of the two earlier volumes was to clarify what power and capitalist modernity entailed. Here, Öcalan presents his stunningly original thesis of the Democratic Civilization, based on his criticism of Capitalist Modernity. Ambitious in scope and encyclopedic in execution, *The Sociology of Freedom* is a one-of-a-kind exploration that reveals the remarkable range of one of the Left's most original thinkers with topics such as existence and freedom, nature and philosophy, anarchism and ecology. Öcalan goes back to the origins of human culture to present a penetrating reinterpretation of the basic problems facing the twenty-first century and an examination of their solutions. Öcalan convincingly argues that industrialism, capitalism, and the nation-state cannot be conquered within the narrow confines of a socialist context.

Recognizing the need for more than just a critique, Öcalan has advanced what is the most radical, far-reaching definition of democracy today and argues that a democratic civilization, as an alternative system, already exists but systemic power and knowledge structures, along with a perverse sectarianism, do not allow it to be seen.

The Sociology of Freedom is a truly monumental work that gives profuse evidence of Öcalan's position as one of the most influential thinkers of our day. It deserves the careful attention of anyone seriously interested in constructive thought or the future of the Left.

Beyond State, Power, and Violence

Abdullah Öcalan
with a Foreword by Andrej Grubačić
Edited by International Initiative

ISBN: 978-1-62963-715-0
$29.95   800 pages

After the dissolution of the PKK (Kurdistan
Workers' Party) in 2002, internal discussions
ran high, and fear and uncertainty about the future of the Kurdish
freedom movement threatened to unravel the gains of decades of
organizing and armed struggle. From his prison cell, Abdullah Öcalan
intervened by penning his most influential work to date: *Beyond State,
Power, and Violence*. With a stunning vision of a freedom movement
centered on women's liberation, democracy, and ecology, Öcalan helped
reinvigorate the Kurdish freedom movement by providing a revolutionary
path forward with what is undoubtedly the furthest-reaching definition
of democracy the world has ever seen. Here, for the first time, is the
highly anticipated English translation of this monumental work.

Beyond State, Power, and Violence is a breathtaking reconnaissance into
life without the state, an essential portrait of the PKK and the Kurdish
freedom movement, and an open blueprint for leftist organizing in
the twenty-first century, written by one of the most vitally important
political luminaries of today.

By carefully analyzing the past and present of the Middle East, Öcalan
evaluates concrete prospects for the Kurdish people and arrives with
his central proposal: recreate the Kurdish freedom movement along
the lines of a new paradigm based on the principles of democratic
confederalism and democratic autonomy. In the vast scope of this
book, Öcalan examines the emergence of hierarchies and eventually
classes in human societies and sketches his alternative, the democratic-
ecological society. This vision, with a theoretical foundation of a
nonviolent means of taking power, has ushered in a new era for the
Kurdish freedom movement while also offering a fresh and indispensible
perspective on the global debate about a new socialism. Öcalan's calls
for nonhierarchical forms of democratic social organization deserve the
careful attention of anyone interested in constructive social thought or
rebuilding society along feminist and ecological lines.

Building Free Life: Dialogues with Öcalan

Edited by International Initiative

ISBN: 978-1-62963-704-4
$20.00   256 pages

From Socrates to Antonio Gramsci, imprisoned philosophers have marked the history of thought and changed how we view power and politics. From his solitary jail cell, Abdullah Öcalan has penned daringly innovative works that give profuse evidence of his position as one of the most significant thinkers of our day. His prison writings have mobilized tens of thousands of people and inspired a revolution in the making in Rojava, northern Syria, while also penetrating the insular walls of academia and triggering debate and reflection among countless scholars.

So how do you engage in a meaningful dialogue with Abdullah Öcalan when he has been held in total isolation since April 2015? You compile a book of essays written by a globally diverse cast of the most imaginative luminaries of our time, send it to Öcalan's jailers, and hope that they deliver it to him.

Featured in this extraordinary volume are over a dozen writers, activists, dreamers, and scholars whose ideas have been investigated in Öcalan's own writings. Now these same people have the unique opportunity to enter into a dialogue with his ideas. Building Free Life is a rich and wholly original exploration of the most critical issues facing humanity today. In the broad sweep of this one-of-a-kind dialogue, the contributors explore topics ranging from democratic confederalism to women's revolution, from the philosophy of history to the crisis of the capitalist system, from religion to Marxism and anarchism, all in an effort to better understand the liberatory social forms that are boldly confronting capitalism and the state.

Contributors include: Shannon Brincat, Radha D'Souza, Mechthild Exo, Damian Gerber, Barry K. Gills, Muriel González Athenas, David Graeber, Andrej Grubačić, John Holloway, Patrick Huff, Donald H. Matthews, Thomas Jeffrey Miley, Antonio Negri, Norman Paech, Ekkehard Sauermann, Fabian Scheidler, Nazan Üstündağ, Immanuel Wallerstein, Peter Lamborn Wilson, and Raúl Zibechi.

The Battle for the Mountain of the Kurds: Self-Determination and Ethnic Cleansing in the Afrin Region of Rojava

Author: Thomas Schmidinger with a Preface by Andrej Grubačić

ISBN: 978-1-62963-651-1
$19.95   192 pages

In early 2018, Turkey invaded the autonomous Kurdish region of Afrin in Syria and is currently threatening to ethnically cleanse the region. Between 2012 and 2018, the "Mountain of the Kurds" (Kurd Dagh) as the area has been called for centuries, had been one of the quietest regions in a country otherwise torn by civil war.

After the outbreak of the Syrian civil war in 2011, the Syrian army withdrew from the region in 2012, enabling the Party of Democratic Union (PYD), the Syrian sister party of Abdullah Öcalan's outlawed Turkish Kurdistan Workers' Party (PKK) to first introduce a Kurdish self-administration and then, in 2014, to establish the Canton Afrin as one of the three parts of the heavily Kurdish Democratic Federation of Northern Syria, which is better known under the name Rojava.

This self-administration—which had seen multiparty municipal and regionwide elections in the summer and autumn of 2017, which included a far-reaching autonomy for a number of ethnic and religious groups, and which had provided a safe haven for up to 300,000 refugees from other parts of Syria—is now at risk of being annihilated by the Turkish invasion and occupation.

Thomas Schmidinger is one of the very few Europeans to have visited the Canton of Afrin. In this book, he gives an account of the history and the present situation of the region. In a number of interviews, he also gives inhabitants of the region from a variety of ethnicities, religions, political orientations, and walks of life the opportunity to speak for themselves. As things stand now, the book might seem to be in danger of becoming an epitaph for the "Mountain of the Kurds," but as the author writes, "the battle for the Mountain of the Kurds is far from over yet."

Capital and Its Discontents: Conversations with Radical Thinkers in a Time of Tumult

Sasha Lilley

ISBN: 978-1-60486-334-5
$20.00   320 pages

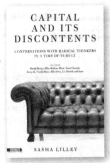

Capitalism is stumbling, empire is faltering, and the planet is thawing. Yet many people are still grasping to understand these multiple crises and to find a way forward to a just future. Into the breach come the essential insights of *Capital and Its Discontents*, which cut through the gristle to get to the heart of the matter about the nature of capitalism and imperialism, capitalism's vulnerabilities at this conjuncture—and what we can do to hasten its demise. Through a series of incisive conversations with some of the most eminent thinkers and political economists on the Left—including David Harvey, Ellen Meiksins Wood, Mike Davis, Leo Panitch, Tariq Ali, and Noam Chomsky—*Capital and Its Discontents* illuminates the dynamic contradictions undergirding capitalism and the potential for its dethroning. At a moment when capitalism as a system is more reviled than ever, here is an indispensable toolbox of ideas for action by some of the most brilliant thinkers of our times.

"*These conversations illuminate the current world situation in ways that are very useful for those hoping to orient themselves and find a way forward to effective individual and collective action. Highly recommended.*"
—Kim Stanley Robinson, *New York Times* bestselling author of the *Mars Trilogy* and *The Years of Rice and Salt*

"*In this fine set of interviews, an A-list of radical political economists demonstrate why their skills are indispensable to understanding today's multiple economic and ecological crises.*"
—Raj Patel, author of *Stuffed and Starved* and *The Value of Nothing*

"*This is an extremely important book. It is the most detailed, comprehensive, and best study yet published on the most recent capitalist crisis and its discontents. Sasha Lilley sets each interview in its context, writing with style, scholarship, and wit about ideas and philosophies.*"
—Andrej Grubačić, radical sociologist and social critic, co-author of *Wobblies and Zapatistas*

Wobblies and Zapatistas: Conversations on Anarchism, Marxism and Radical History

Staughton Lynd and Andrej Grubačić

ISBN: 978-1-60486-041-2
$20.00   300 pages

Wobblies and Zapatistas offers the reader an encounter between two generations and two traditions. Andrej Grubačić is an anarchist from the Balkans. Staughton Lynd is a lifelong pacifist, influenced by Marxism. They meet in dialogue in an effort to bring together the anarchist and Marxist traditions, to discuss the writing of history by those who make it, and to remind us of the idea that "my country is the world." Encompassing a Left libertarian perspective and an emphatically activist standpoint, these conversations are meant to be read in the clubs and affinity groups of the new Movement.

The authors accompany us on a journey through modern revolutions, direct actions, anti-globalist counter summits, Freedom Schools, Zapatista cooperatives, Haymarket and Petrograd, Hanoi and Belgrade, 'intentional' communities, wildcat strikes, early Protestant communities, Native American democratic practices, the Workers' Solidarity Club of Youngstown, occupied factories, self-organized councils and soviets, the lives of forgotten revolutionaries, Quaker meetings, antiwar movements, and prison rebellions. Neglected and forgotten moments of interracial self-activity are brought to light. The book invites the attention of readers who believe that a better world, on the other side of capitalism and state bureaucracy, may indeed be possible.

"There's no doubt that we've lost much of our history. It's also very clear that those in power in this country like it that way. Here's a book that shows us why. It demonstrates not only that another world is possible, but that it already exists, has existed, and shows an endless potential to burst through the artificial walls and divisions that currently imprison us. An exquisite contribution to the literature of human freedom, and coming not a moment too soon."
—David Graeber, author of *Fragments of an Anarchist Anthropology* and *Direct Action: An Ethnography*

Asylum for Sale: Profit and Protest in the Migration Industry

Edited by Siobhán McGuirk &
Adrienne Pine with a Foreword by
Seth M. Holmes

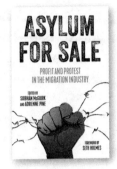

ISBN: 978-1-62963-782-2
Price: $27.95   368 pages

This explosive new volume brings together a lively cast of academics, activists, journalists, artists, and people directly impacted by asylum regimes to explain how current practices of asylum align with the neoliberal moment and to present their transformative visions for alternative systems and processes.

Through essays, artworks, photographs, infographics, and illustrations, *Asylum for Sale: Profit and Protest in the Migration Industry* regards the global asylum regime as an industry characterized by profit-making activity: brokers who facilitate border crossings for a fee; contractors and firms that erect walls, fences, and watchtowers while lobbying governments for bigger "security" budgets; corporations running private detention centers and "managing" deportations; private lawyers charging exorbitant fees; "expert" witnesses; and NGO staff establishing careers while placing asylum seekers into new regimes of monitored vulnerability.

Asylum for Sale challenges readers to move beyond questions of legal, moral, and humanitarian obligations that dominate popular debates regarding asylum seekers. Digging deeper, the authors focus on processes and actors often overlooked in mainstream analyses and on the trends increasingly rendering asylum available only to people with financial and cultural capital. Probing every aspect of the asylum process from crossings to aftermaths, the book provides an in-depth exploration of complex, international networks, policies, and norms that impact people seeking asylum around the world.

"As the frontiers of disaster capitalism expand, the same systems that drive migration are finding ever-more harrowing ways to criminalize and exploit the displaced. This book is part of how we fight back: connecting the extraordinary stories and insights of people studying, personally navigating, and creatively resisting the global asylum industry. An unparalleled resource."
—Naomi Klein, author of *On Fire: The Burning Case for the Green New D*

In, Against, and Beyond Capitalism: The San Francisco Lectures

John Holloway
with a Preface by Andrej Grubačić

ISBN: 978-1-62963-109-7
$14.95   112 pages

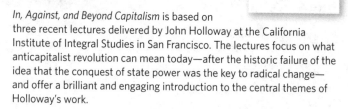

In, Against, and Beyond Capitalism is based on three recent lectures delivered by John Holloway at the California Institute of Integral Studies in San Francisco. The lectures focus on what anticapitalist revolution can mean today—after the historic failure of the idea that the conquest of state power was the key to radical change—and offer a brilliant and engaging introduction to the central themes of Holloway's work.

The lectures take as their central challenge the idea that "We Are the Crisis of Capital and Proud of It." This runs counter to many leftist assumptions that the capitalists are to blame for the crisis, or that crisis is simply the expression of the bankruptcy of the system. The only way to see crisis as the possible threshold to a better world is to understand the failure of capitalism as the face of the push of our creative force. This poses a theoretical challenge. The first lecture focuses on the meaning of "We," the second on the understanding of capital as a system of social cohesion that systematically frustrates our creative force, and the third on the proposal that we are the crisis of this system of cohesion.

"His Marxism is premised on another form of logic, one that affirms movement, instability, and struggle. This is a movement of thought that affirms the richness of life, particularity (non-identity) and 'walking in the opposite direction'; walking, that is, away from exploitation, domination, and classification. Without contradictory thinking in, against, and beyond the capitalist society, capital once again becomes a reified object, a thing, and not a social relation that signifies transformation of a useful and creative activity (doing) into (abstract) labor. Only open dialectics, a right kind of thinking for the wrong kind of world, non-unitary thinking without guarantees, is able to assist us in our contradictory struggle for a world free of contradiction."
—Andrej Grubačić, from his Preface

"Holloway's work is infectiously optimistic."
—Steven Poole, the *Guardian* (UK)

Re-enchanting the World: Feminism and the Politics of the Commons

Silvia Federici
with a Foreword by Peter Linebaugh

ISBN: 978-1-62963-569-9
$19.95   240 pages

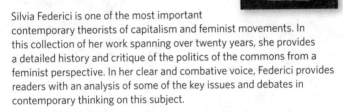

Silvia Federici is one of the most important contemporary theorists of capitalism and feminist movements. In this collection of her work spanning over twenty years, she provides a detailed history and critique of the politics of the commons from a feminist perspective. In her clear and combative voice, Federici provides readers with an analysis of some of the key issues and debates in contemporary thinking on this subject.

Drawing on rich historical research, she maps the connections between the previous forms of enclosure that occurred with the birth of capitalism and the destruction of the commons and the "new enclosures" at the heart of the present phase of global capitalist accumulation. Considering the commons from a feminist perspective, this collection centers on women and reproductive work as crucial to both our economic survival and the construction of a world free from the hierarchies and divisions capital has planted in the body of the world proletariat. Federici is clear that the commons should not be understood as happy islands in a sea of exploitative relations but rather autonomous spaces from which to challenge the existing capitalist organization of life and labor.

"*Silvia Federici's theoretical capacity to articulate the plurality that fuels the contemporary movement of women in struggle provides a true toolbox for building bridges between different features and different people.*"
—Massimo De Angelis, professor of political economy, University of East London

"*Silvia Federici's work embodies an energy that urges us to rejuvenate struggles against all types of exploitation and, precisely for that reason, her work produces a common: a common sense of the dissidence that creates a community in struggle.*"
—Maria Mies, coauthor of *Ecofeminism*

Crossroads: I Live Where I Like: A Graphic History

Koni Benson. Illustrated byAndré Trantraal, Nathan Trantraal, and Ashley E. Marais, and with a Foreword by Robin D.G. Kelley

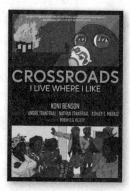

ISBN: 978-1-62963-835-5
$20.00   168 pages

Drawn by South African political cartoonists the Trantraal brothers and Ashley Marais, *Crossroads: I Live Where I Like* is a graphic nonfiction history of women-led movements at the forefront of the struggle for land, housing, water, education, and safety in Cape Town over half a century. Drawing on over sixty life narratives, it tells the story of women who built and defended Crossroads, the only informal settlement that successfully resisted the apartheid bulldozers in Cape Town. The story follows women's organized resistance from the peak of apartheid in the 1970s to ongoing struggles for decent shelter today. Importantly, this account was workshopped with contemporary housing activists and women's collectives who chose the most urgent and ongoing themes they felt spoke to and clarified challenges against segregation, racism, violence, and patriarchy standing between the legacy of the colonial and apartheid past and a future of freedom still being fought for.

Presenting dramatic visual representations of many personalities and moments in the daily life of this township, the book presents a thoughtful and thorough chronology, using archival newspapers, posters, photography, pamphlets, and newsletters to further illustrate the significance of the struggles at Crossroads for the rest of the city and beyond. This collaboration has produced a beautiful, captivating, accessible, forgotten, and in many ways uncomfortable history of Cape Town that has yet to be acknowledged.

"Crossroads is, quite simply, beautiful. It is intellectual and appealing and everything one could hope for from this kind of project. It is a meaningful engagement with a deeply troubling and enormously significant past. Not only does it weave text and images together to their best effect, but this is also one of the most insightful studies of urban history and social movements in any medium."
—Trevor Getz, professor of African history, San Francisco State University; author of *Abina and the Important Men: A Graphic History*; and series editor of the Oxford University Press's Uncovering History series